Contents

Language development	Speaking	Study skills	Unit outcomes
Notice and study binomials (*give and take, all or nothing* etc.) to use the phrases correctly Use modal verbs to express different levels of directness	Identify and use intonation patterns expressing attitude Review and use phrases for interrupting others Prepare and participate in a meeting about forming a study group	Learn how to effectively participate in small groups	**Listen to infer attitude** in the context of formal and informal conversations Listen to **identify the stages of a process** Prepare and **contribute to an informal meeting and discussion**
Recognize and use prepositional verbs Recognize and use phrasal verbs	Identify the linking /r/ sound to spot word boundaries and listen more effectively Expand and practice phrases for agreeing and disagreeing in formal or informal contexts Plan and take part in a class debate about games	Understand the importance of critical thinking skills in professional and everyday life	Listen to **identify key information in an argument** **Select key information for summaries and notes** Plan and take part in **a seminar debate**
Notice and practice phrases and structures expressing approximation Use particularizer and exclusive adverbs to give specific information	Recognize and follow juncture in connected speech Attribute and identify sources of information in your presentations Plan, conduct, and present the findings of a survey on memory	Discuss and explore techniques for listening to extended lectures	Practice **organizing data** gathered from texts Identify and critique **sources of information** in listening and speaking Conduct and present **a survey and its findings**
Use nominalization to achieve a more academic and formal tone Notice and use phrases and grammar structures for future predictions	Identify and recognize word stress in word families Change topics, return to earlier points, and stay with your topic to manage conversations Brainstorm, prepare, and present a risk assessment for one of three scenarios	Compare and reflect on your skills and attitudes to critical thinking	**Anticipate conclusions while you listen** based on reasoning and evidence Identify **illustrative examples** in listening Prepare and present **a risk assessment** for a hypothetical future scenario
Recognize and make use of positive and negative connotations Notice and study academic verbs to focus on specific meanings of actions	Notice and use stress patterns to contrast information Practice words and phrases for supporting your proposals when speaking Plan and present a proposal for an urban-related project	Think and talk about ways of recording your achievements	**Listen for the logical order** of lectures or presentations Practice **critical listening to evaluate** according to chosen criteria Prepare and present **a project proposal** related to an urban issue

Contents

Contents

Language development	Speaking	Study skills	Unit outcomes
Create emphasis or stress key information by using inversion Recognize and explore collocations with *way*	Identify and use pauses for dramatic emphasis Explore and practice techniques used to emphasize important information Brainstorm, plan, and deliver a three-minute speech about an influential person	Discuss and recognize ways to identify the author's position in texts	Listen to **assess the validity of a speaker's sources** Listen to **identify source citations** Prepare and deliver **a three-minute speech about an influential person**
Identify and explore attitude adverbials (*naturally, oddly enough* etc.) for more effective listening and speaking Study and record abstract nouns	Recognize word stress in abstract nouns Make suggestions, check facts, and ask key questions to negotiate better Brainstorm, discuss, and negotiate plans for a study program	Compare and talk about ways of organizing your personal study online	Listen to **distinguish facts from opinions** Listen to **identify statements in need of justification** **Prepare and negotiate a study program proposal**
Review and practice ways of talking about change Review and identify gradable and non-gradable adjectives	Use and notice tonic prominence in intonation patterns Practice words and phrases for adding points to an argument Prepare, plan, and participate in a debate about digital change in education	Distinguish between arguments and disagreements in academic contexts	Listen for **exaggerated and maximizing language** Listen to **identify implicit assumptions** in texts Research and take part in **an organized debate**
Review and explore irregular plurals in English Work with concordance data to study words in their contexts	Recognize and use intonation patterns that express hesitation or doubt Develop phrases to soften criticism in discussions Brainstorm, produce, and share a promotional message about water economy	Compare and discuss techniques for performing well on exams	Listen to **distinguish arguments and counter-arguments** **Make use of visual aids and diagrams** when listening Prepare and share **a short persuasive message**
Recognize and use hedging and boosting techniques to manage the strength of your arguments Identify and use linkers to join arguments effectively	Notice catenation and linking in connected speech to identify words properly Use reformulating and monitoring language to check and manage conflicting statements or positions Brainstorm, research, and perform a conflict-based role-play	Learn to use categorising techniques to organize information for debates and reports	Listen to **recognize strengths and weaknesses of an argument** Listen for **consistent order in speaker's contributions** and for **inconsistencies** Prepare and participate in **a role-play exercise** based on a conflict

To the Student

Academic success requires more than memorizing information—it takes skills. A successful student not only understands the lesson in one class, but can also apply knowledge to future classes and to situations outside the classroom.

Each unit of *Skillful* presents one main topic about life, examined from two different academic disciplines. As you work through the unit, you will see how these two very different aspects of the topic work together to inform our understanding of a profound concept.

To explore the topic, each unit presents:

- Two texts that explore very different aspects of the topic. The texts are similar to the ones you would find in a university course, although the types of texts are quite varied—reports, essays, debates, radio programs, and so on.
- For each text, a specific skill to help you understand the information and then produce your own text on a similar topic
- Vocabulary and grammar skills to help you understand what you hear and then compose and present your own academically appropriate texts
- A pronunciation skill to help you listen more effectively and communicate more clearly
- Critical thinking skills to help you engage with the topic intellectually
- A study skill to improve your ability to learn, remember, and apply information to your life

To successfully use this book, use these strategies:

- **Come to class prepared to learn.** This means that you should show up on time and well fed, well rested, and prepared with the proper materials (paper/pen or laptop/tablet, textbook, completed homework, and so on).
- **Ask questions and interact.** Learning a language is not passive. You need to actively participate. Help your classmates, and let them help you. It is easier to learn a language with other people.
- **Practice!** Do each exercise a few times, with different partners. Memorize and use new language. Collaborate with classmates outside of class and practice both skills and language.
- **Review your work.** Look over the skills, grammar, and vocabulary from previous units. Study a little bit each day, not just before tests.
- **Be an independent learner.** Look for opportunities to study and practice English outside of class. Read and listen for pleasure, and use the Internet in English. Find and share information about the different unit topics with your classmates.

Remember that learning skills, like learning a language, takes time and practice. Be patient with yourself, but do not forget to set goals. Check your progress, and be proud of your success!

I hope you enjoy using *Skillful*!

Dorothy E. Zemach
Series Consultant

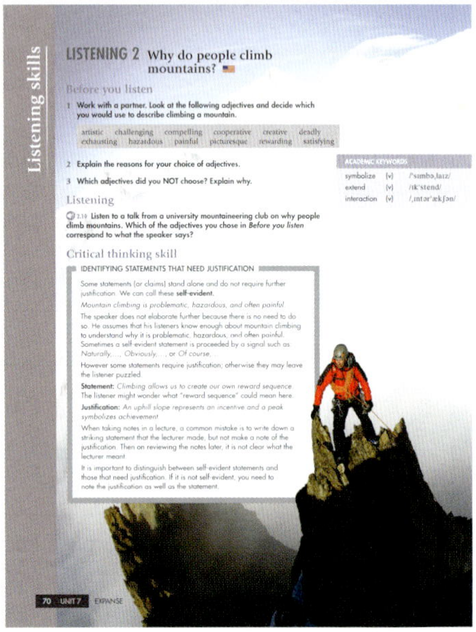

UNIT 1

Gathering

CRITICAL THINKING	Inferring a speaker's attitude Applying a theory to other situations
LANGUAGE DEVELOPMENT	Binomials Modal verbs and levels of directness
PRONUNCIATION	Intonation and attitude
SPEAKING	Interrupting

Discussion point

Discuss these questions with a partner.

1 Think about the past week. Which groups of people have you been with? Check the categories below. Can you think of any other groups you spent time with? Compare with a partner.

☐ social club ☐ fellow students ☐ close family ☐ extended family
☐ work colleagues ☐ teammates ☐ former school friends ☐ volunteer group

2 Are you someone who participates a lot in a group, likes to be the leader, or prefers to watch and listen? What kinds of people do you like being in a group with?

3 What types of meeting have you attended (for example, school meeting, team meeting, club meeting, work meeting)? What were they for?

Vocabulary preview

Read the information about lectures and seminars, and fill in the spaces with the words in the box.

chaotic	coordinator	figure out	handouts	nominated	objectives	participation	professor

Leading the lecture or seminar—key tips

The lecture or seminar, whether it's face-to-face or online, remains a key aspect of learning for almost all college students. While it's often the (1) ______________ or teacher in charge of delivering the information, sometimes students are also charged with leading a seminar. Here are some tips for an effective session.

- If speakers have a lot to say, consider asking a (2) ______________ to distribute (3) ______________ with extra notes that people can take home with them.
- Is there a (4) ______________ speaker? In many group discussions, one person leads the talk. However, this should not exclude individual (5) ______________.
- Are the (6) ______________ for the seminar clear? If they are not, the audience may be left trying to (7) ______________ the purpose of the meeting.
- Avoid a long slideshow. Too much information can come across as (8) ______________ and overload people. Feature only the most important information.
- Minimize the chance of interruptions. Ask the audience to mute their phones, and allocate a set time—usually at the end—for questions.

LISTENING 1 Three meetings

Before you listen

Look at the following pairs of words about meeting types. How are they similar? How are they different? Think about speakers, purpose, interaction patterns, and technology.

1 a lecture / a seminar
2 a summit / a rally
3 an audio conference / a webinar
4 a get-together / an interview

Listening

1 1.02 **Listen to *Three meetings*. What type of meeting is each one? Choose from the list in *Before you listen*. What is the purpose of each meeting?**

2 1.02 **Listen again and answer these questions.**

Meeting 1

1 What is the professor's course about?

2 How many dos and don'ts does the professor cover?

Meeting 2

3 What three interruptions occur at the beginning of the second meeting?

4 How does the speaker suggest splitting the workload?

Meeting 3

5 What benefits to joining the society does the speaker talk about?

6 What term does the lead speaker use to imply that the group is freely accessible?

ACADEMIC KEYWORDS

aspect	(n)	/'æspekt/
characterize	(v)	/'kerəktə,raɪz/
integrate	(v)	/'ɪntə,greɪt/

Listening skills

Critical thinking skill

INFERRING A SPEAKER'S ATTITUDE

We infer a speaker's attitude toward a topic from a range of factors. These might include: context, relationship between speakers, gender, age, setting, word choice, our knowledge of the speaker, the speaker's body language, and the speaker's intonation.

It is often the final element—intonation—that gives us most clues about a speaker's attitude. For example, a speaker may use very formal and polite language, but convey a different attitude, or even sound rude, due to his/her intonation (cf. p. 14).

1 1.02 **Listen again. For each meeting, select the adjective that best describes the attitude of the main speaker. Think of context, word choice, and intonation.**

1 The professor
  a upset **b** abrupt **c** passionate

2 The woman in charge of the meeting
  a nervous **b** irritated **c** shy

3 The lead speaker from the debating society
  a insincere **b** impatient **c** afraid

2 **Work with a partner. Compare your answers. What evidence can you give in support of each answer?**

In exercise 1, I think the best adjective to describe the professor is "passionate." I think he's passionate because of the expressions he uses, such as "the most important." His intonation also shows his attitude because his voice rises when he describes the various elements of the course.

Developing critical thinking

Discuss these questions in a group.

1 Have you been in situations like those presented in the listening? How did you feel when interruptions took place?

2 How is technology changing the way we interact? Do you think everyone will eventually only hold meetings, classes, and lectures remotely?

3 Have you ever taken an online course? What did you think of it? Can you think of one advantage and one disadvantage of replacing face-to-face lectures with online lectures?

LISTENING 2 Getting from *you and me*, to *we*

Before you listen

1 **Have you heard the expression "the whole is greater than the sum of its parts"? What does it mean? Is there a similar expression in your language?**

2 **Think of a time when you were part of a successful or unsuccessful group. For example, an athletic team, club, or class. What made the group successful/unsuccessful—the people, the venue, the timing ...?**

Listening

1 1.03 **Listen to some people talking and answer these questions.**

1 What type of meeting is this?
2 Who are the speakers and what is their relationship?
3 What is "group dynamics"?

2 **Which best describes the situation?**

a A presentation on online study methods
b A discussion on the stages of working together
c An example of poor group dynamics

Critical thinking skill

APPLYING A THEORY TO OTHER SITUATIONS

A theory is a set of ideas that helps to explain why something happens in a particular way. In academia, a theory can be an idea or a set of ideas that we believe to be true, but might not have been proven.

When a theory is introduced, for example in a lecture, usually an example is given to show how the theory works. To show our understanding of a theory, it is important that we are able to apply it to other situations as well.

ACADEMIC KEYWORDS

conform	(v)	/kən'fɔrm/
originally	(adv)	/ə'rɪdʒən(ə)li/
relevance	(n)	/'reləvəns/

1 1.03 **Listen again. Identify which stage of the theory of group dynamics in the box is being referred to in each sentence. Some stages are used more than once.**

adjourning	forming	norming	performing	storming

1 It's important that there is clear leadership and direction. ______________
2 Individual members begin to voice their differences. ______________
3 The team leader takes more of a back seat. ______________
4 This may result in open conflict within the group. ______________
5 A bit like the calm after the storm. ______________
6 The members of the group can move forward. ______________
7 A lot is achieved during this stage. ______________
8 It's about moving on. ______________

2 **Read sentences from people's experiences with groups. Applying group dynamics theory, which stage of group development are they going through?**

1 "I think we're all a bit nervous about talking to each other after what happened last week. But at least we can get some work done this time."
2 "Our team has been playing together really well, and I just don't know what I'm going to do when the season finishes in two days."
3 "I was happy to see a friend here, so I sat next to her. Nobody really talks to each other, and we're all a bit shy."
4 "Today was a great class. I felt as if the students really pulled together and we got through a tremendous amount of material. They had lots of questions, and everyone felt great."

Developing critical thinking

1 **Discuss these questions in a group.**

1 Do you think Bruce Tuckman's theory of group dynamics is a good description of how people work together? Have you been in a group that has been through the various stages in the theory? Think back to the experiences you talked about in the *Before you listen* section.
2 Imagine you were in a group that was in the storming stage. Describe two specific problems that could happen during that stage. Then make two suggestions on how to get beyond that stage.

2 **Think about the ideas from *Listening 1* and *Listening 2*, and discuss these questions in a group.**

1 "Knowledge about how groups work is vital for people who want to be leaders." Think of one argument for and one argument against this statement.
2 In what situations do you think people work better alone than with a group? Think of three examples and tell a partner.

References for *Getting from* you and me, *to* we:

Forsyth, D. *Group Dynamics 5th edition*. Cengage Learning, 2009.

Tuckman, B. (1965) "Developmental sequence in small groups" Psychological Bulletin 63 (6): 384–99. The article was reprinted in *Group Facilitation: A Research and Applications Journal*—Number 3, Spring 2001, and is available as a Word document: http://dennislearningcenter.osu.edu/references/GROUP%20DEV%20ARTICLE.doc. Accessed February 14, 2013.

Language development

BINOMIALS

A binomial is a pair of words that are joined by a conjunction and always go in the same order. For example: *bread and butter* (NOT *butter and bread*).

Binomials can be pairs of nouns (*bread and butter*), verbs (*see and do*), or adjectives (*sad, but true*).

1 Match the words in A with the words in B to make binomials.

A		B
all		clear
cut		downs
give	and	dried
loud		effort
pure	or	nothing
show		simple
time		take
ups		tell

2 Look at the following extracts from meetings or classes. Fill in the spaces with the binomials in exercise 1. Use the correct word order and conjunction.

1 We'd like to thank you for all your ________________ with the company. We really appreciate all you've done.

2 Next week we are going to have a(n) ________________ activity. Everyone has to bring a typical item from his or her country.

3 Well, I think the message is getting across ________________. We all understand.

4 The deadline for this project is tomorrow, so we have to make a special effort. It's really a(n) ________________ affair right now.

5 The company has been through its ________________, but the directors think we will emerge from this even stronger.

6 I know we said we would solve this problem in one meeting, but I don't think it's as ________________ as that.

7 Our main aim is to make student life as good as possible on campus, ________________.

8 Our next meeting will be in two months, ________________ a day or two.

MODAL VERBS AND LEVELS OF DIRECTNESS

The choice of modal verb to express a function can change depending on the situation and also the meaning the speaker wishes to convey. For example, some modals can sound very direct, but changing the modal form (*could* instead of *can*, *would* instead of *will*, *might* instead of *may*) can soften a statement and make it less direct. In more formal situations, or to sound less direct, speakers may also change the sentence structure, or modify a modal verb with adverbs, such as *possibly*, *probably*, *ideally*, and *please*.

Compare these sentences:

*We **must** start the meeting now.* (very direct, almost an order)

***Could** we start the meeting now?* (less direct than *can*, a request)

***Shall** we start the meeting now?* (indirect, formal suggestion)

***Might** we **possibly** start the meeting now?* (indirect, almost tentative)

However, verb choice is not the only way to achieve directness. Other factors such as intonation (cf. p. 14) also play a role.

1 Rate the level of directness of each sentence below on a scale of 1–5, with 5 = very direct, 1 = very indirect.

1 We may as well get started then. ___
2 See if he's online. ___
3 Shall we take a break? ___
4 Can I possibly add something here? ___
5 Listen everybody! ___
6 Would you take notes, Peter? ___
7 You mustn't use that word in class. ___
8 We won't leave until we get an answer. ___

2 In what settings might you hear each of the expressions in exercise 1?

3 Work with a partner. Change each sentence in exercise 1 to alter the level of directness of the sentence.

4 Look at the following situations. For each situation, think of two different ways, direct and indirect, that you could express yourself.

1 You are in a meeting. You need to leave early.

Direct: Can I go early? I have another appointment.

Indirect: Excuse me, might it be possible for me to leave early? I have another appointment.

2 You want to ask a question in class.
3 A new student looks a bit lost.
4 You and some classmates want to meet after class and do something.
5 A phone keeps ringing during class.

SPEAKING Planning a study group

You are going to learn about how intonation can be used to show a speaker's attitude. You will also learn how to interrupt another person politely. Then you are going to use these skills to participate in a meeting about planning a study group.

Pronunciation skill

INTONATION AND ATTITUDE

Intonation is the way the voice rises and falls when we speak; it is *how* we say something, not *what* we say. Understanding intonation is an important skill for establishing the emotions, thoughts, and intentions of the speaker.

Depending on a speaker's intonation, various positive and negative attitudes can be conveyed, such as boredom, interest, enthusiasm, surprise, irritation, anger, sarcasm, etc.

I'm really looking forward to the meeting. (normal intonation)

I'm really looking forward to the meeting. (stress on *really* and downward intonation at the end represents sarcasm)

Don't forget that intonation doesn't operate alone in suggesting attitude. Pauses, pitch, tone, and speed all play a role, too.

1 1.04 **Listen to three different versions of the dialogue below. For each version, choose the words that best describe each speaker's attitude.**

A: I'm sorry, but I can't come to the meeting today.

B: Oh, OK. We'll have the meeting next week then.

anger indifference sarcasm surprise suspicion worry

2 1.04 **Listen again to the three versions of the dialogue. Then practice the dialogues with a partner. Copy the intonation in each version.**

Speaking skill

INTERRUPTING

In a situation where many people are speaking and you want to say something, you may have to interrupt the other speaker(s). It is important to know when and how to interrupt another person appropriately and politely. In formal situations, you can use *Excuse me*, or *Sorry*, and we would usually add another phrase to ask for permission to speak.

Excuse me, do you mind if I interrupt? *Excuse me, may I say something, please?*

Sorry (to interrupt), but would you mind if I said something (at this point)?

In informal situations, you can be more abrupt.

Hang on. *Wait a minute/second/moment.* *Can I say something?*

1 **Complete the interrupting phrases with the missing words.**

1 ____________ to ____________, but …

2 ____________ I ____________ something here?

3 ____________ you ____________ if I say ____________ here?

2 **With a partner, take turns to start a topic and interrupt.**

SPEAKING TASK

BRAINSTORM

Work with a partner. What is a study group?

Look at these ways of studying together outside of class. Which ones have you tried? Which ones would you like to try? Are there other ways you can think of?

Meeting to practice talking in English	Setting up an online webpage to study
Exchanging useful websites	Reviewing past lessons together
Writing emails to each other in English	Studying together for exams
Participating in an online discussion forum	

PLAN

1 1.05 Listen to some American college students planning a study group. Answer these questions.

1. How many people will be in the study group?
2. Where will they meet?
3. How long will they meet for, and how often will they meet?

2 1.05 Listen again. Take notes on the use of modals in various functions, the intonation of the speakers, and the language they used when they interrupted each other. Discuss your notes with a partner, and say whether you think their study group will be successful.

3 Imagine you want to start a study group. Think about:

- What is the purpose of your study group?
- What is the best mode of interaction for your study group? Online, face-to-face …
- Should your study group have a leader? How will you nominate the leader?
- How will you monitor if the study group is effective or not?

SPEAK

Work with another pair. Have an initial meeting about forming a study group. Share your ideas about the best way for a study group to work. Take turns speaking. Interrupt other speakers appropriately to make suggestions, offers, or requests.

SHARE

Tell the class what plans you have for a study group. Make a strategy and set a schedule to put your plans into practice!

Study skills

STUDY SKILLS Speaking in groups

Getting started

Discuss these questions with a partner.

1 In your previous English classes, how much speaking in groups did you have to do?
2 Did you find it easy or difficult?
3 Why do so many English learners say speaking is the most difficult skill? Think of three reasons.

Scenario

Read about Jemal's experience as an advanced student speaking in a university seminar, and think about how he could participate more.

Jemal has reached an advanced level of English and really knows his grammar and vocabulary. He has always received high grades in English and can do very well on written exams. In his previous English classes he didn't have to speak that much, but he was always able to communicate his ideas where necessary and was very careful not to make mistakes.

However, his new teacher this year expects the students to do a lot of small group discussions. Jemal has been quiet week after week. He's not accustomed to the teacher not lecturing. One time he did participate, but the others in his group didn't really understand what he was saying, so he gave up.

In addition, for the first time, he feels shy and worried about his language level. There are others in the group who are very confident in their speaking. He worries that he will make a mistake and people will laugh. Sometimes Jemal is about to say something, but someone else in the group gets there first. Sometimes he's not sure if it's his turn to speak.

Finally, Jemal has noticed that the teacher is very happy when his group is talking, even if he isn't saying anything. As a result, Jemal has decided the best thing to do is listen and avoid attention.

Consider it

Read these tips about speaking in tutorials, seminars, and small groups. Which tips do you think would be most useful for Jemal? Which have you tried?

1 **Agree with the last speaker**. The easiest way of getting into a conversation and keeping it going is to agree with the last speaker. Say something such as *That's right, Yes, OK,* or even just *Uhuh*. Even if you don't know what to add you can say something like: *I was thinking that myself* or *That's a very good point.*
2 **Add information.** If everyone just said *That's right* the tutorial would stop. Try adding to the last speaker's remark as well. Phrases like *Yes, that reminds me …* or *I have another example of this …*
3 **Ask for information.** If you really don't have anything to add, but you have heard something interesting, ask another speaker for information. Ask *What do you mean by …?* or *Can you tell me another example …?*
4 **Give your opinion.** Giving your opinion helps keep a discussion going. Opinions are usually introduced with phrases such as *I think …, It seems to me …, In my opinion …* Many people use language to show they are not sure, for example, *I was wondering if …, Do you think that perhaps …,* or *Just supposing that …*
5 **Disagree with something.** Part of academic tutorial or seminar discussions is disagreeing with a point someone has just made. Putting doubts into words is one way of finding out what you think yourself and thinking of new ideas as a group.
6 **Show interest.** You can keep the conversation going by showing interest and using phrases such as *Really? Is that true?*
7 **Learn from others**. When you are in a small group discussion or tutorial, pay attention to ways that other students join in. How do they get a turn to talk? How do they show that they are listening to each other? What words do they use to question other people's ideas? What words show they are not sure if their own ideas are right? Paying attention to this will help you adapt to the style of the group.

Over to you

Discuss these questions with a partner.

1 Do you think you participate enough in group discussions?
2 Which of the tips in *Consider it* do you think are most useful?
3 Do you have any other suggestions on how you can participate more actively in discussions?

UNIT 2

Games

CRITICAL THINKING	Identifying key information in an argument Selecting information for notes and summaries
LANGUAGE DEVELOPMENT	Prepositional verbs Phrasal verbs
PRONUNCIATION	Identifying the linking /r/
SPEAKING	Agreeing and disagreeing—degrees of formality

Discussion point

Discuss these questions with a partner.

1 Make a list of games that you played when you were little and then in your early teens. Which were your favorite games? Which of these games do you still play?

2 Which types of game do you think can be educational and which are not? Explain your reasons.

3 Do you prefer single-player games or those you play in a team? Why?

Vocabulary preview

Read and complete the text about video games.

addiction	dopamine	likelihood	motivate
neurologists	reward	stimulating	ultimatum

The elements of a video game are similar to a movie. A successful video game needs (1) ______________ elements in order to (2) ______________ a player to return to the game again and again. Visual appeal increases the (3) ______________ of a game's success. Players also need a sufficient level of challenge, which can be increased by (4) ______________ elements such as gaining extra points or lives. (5) ______________ have pinpointed an increase in (6) ______________ levels when a person feels emotionally fulfilled. At an extreme, a craving for reward can lead to gaming (7) ______________. This condition can be a serious problem, causing gamers to lose touch with reality. In extreme cases, family or friends may give gaming addicts an (8) ______________: quit gaming or face a punishment.

LISTENING 1 Video games: Lessons for life

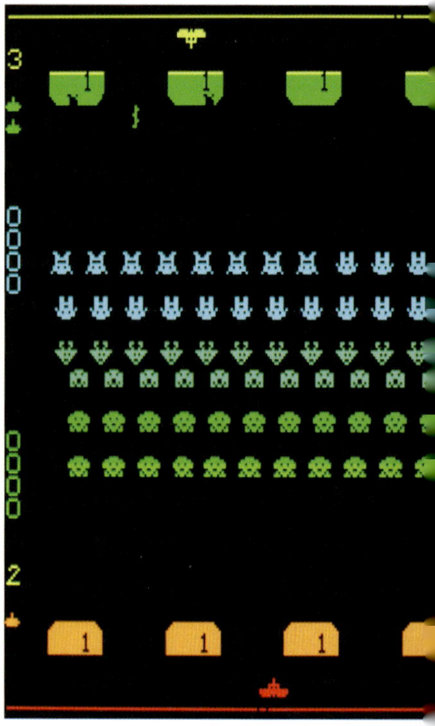

Before you listen

Read the statements on video games and indicate whether you think they are true or false. Justify your reasons.

1 Video game addiction cannot be cured. ___
2 Studying a person's behavior while playing a video game can help us understand how people learn. ___
3 Playing video games cannot teach you any skills that you can use in real life. ___
4 Gaming cannot make you a better student. ___
5 Playing video games regularly can help you become a better driver. ___
6 Children who play video games show enhanced creativity. ___

Listening

1 1.06 **Listen to a university lecture on video games. Check whether the statements in *Before you listen* are true, false, or not given according to the speaker.**

2 **The five things we can learn from video games, as discussed in the lecture, are listed below. Put them in the order that the lecturer mentioned them (1–5).**

enhanced visual attention ___ learning from feedback ___ creativity ___
reward for effort ___ achieving long- and short-term aims ___

ACADEMIC KEYWORDS

enhance	(v)	/ɪn'hæns/
significantly	(adv)	/sɪg'nɪfɪkəntli/
stimulus	(n)	/'stɪmjələs/

Critical thinking skill

IDENTIFYING KEY INFORMATION IN AN ARGUMENT

An academic argument can be defined as a point of view with a line of reasoning to support it. A speaker presenting an argument will usually present a series of points in stages. When a speaker does this, it helps you to identify that the points are key information in the argument.

1 The point is stated in general terms.
Children who play video games tend to be more creative.

2 An example is given.
Child gamers become more creative in classroom tasks such as drawing pictures and writing stories.

3 Reasons or evidence are given to support the main argument (cf. p. 67).
Psychology professor Linda Jackson's study is the first to provide clear evidence of this.

4 The point is summarized.
Regardless of gender or type of game played, there was a clear increase in creativity.

1 1.06 **Listen to the lecture again. Which five of these sentences contain key information in the argument?**

1 Many people enjoy playing video games.
2 Video games offer us very strong emotional rewards.
3 Understanding how video games work can give us a greater insight into how learning takes place.
4 Scientists have found a strong relationship between how the brain responds to rewards and the likelihood of learning.
5 You may gain an enormous number of points, which allows you to continue the game comfortably.
6 Dopamine helps focus our attention; it enhances our potential for learning.
7 Playing video games enhances our visual skills.

2 **For each group of sentences, decide which are key points stated in general terms (*K*), and which are examples, reasons or evidence to support the main argument (*E*).**

1 Video games … gives us greater insight into how learning takes place. ___
Scientists have found a strong relationship between how the brain responds to rewards and the likelihood of learning. ___
When someone receives a reward, a part of the brain, is activated [and] this in turn increases dopamine uptake … [which] enhances our potential for learning. ___

2 The first point is learning to achieve long-term and short-term aims. ___
In a typical game, you have to complete a number of small tasks, and you are generally rewarded for each. ___
As a student you can be taught to organise your work into smaller tasks. ___

3 In a game we work towards a goal, choosing actions and experiencing consequences along the way. ___
You may gain an enormous amount of points, which allows you to continue the game comfortably. However, you could easily lose everything. ___
No one can learn unless they are able to connect consequences to actions. ___

Developing critical thinking

Read this sentence. Which point in *Critical thinking skill* exercise 2 does it summarize?

This can be the key to drawing attention to how you can achieve real life long-term goals such as finish secondary school or get a university degree. ___

Produce a summary for the other points from exercise 2. In a group, evaluate the effectiveness of each other's summary lines.

Listening skills

LISTENING 2 Game theory

Before you listen

Read the course outline about game theory and fill in the spaces with the words in the box.

cooperate	decisions	diplomacy	economics	engage	losses	mathematical	negotiations

Game theory is the study of decision-making using (1) ______________ formulae. It looks at how people act in games or scenarios involving gains and (2) ______________.

Ever since modern game theory achieved prominence in the mid-twentieth century, it has been instrumental in helping people understand how and why we make (3) ______________. Through game theory we can gain insights into all activities in which humans (4) ______________ or compete. These activities include biology, computer science, politics, agriculture, and (5) ______________. In fact, the choices that affect our financial world are some of the most important that are affected by game theory.

Here are some examples of how knowledge of game theory operates in the world: It helps decision-makers in corporations during complex (6) ______________. It plays a crucial role in international (7) ______________ and military strategy. It can even be seen at work in the interactions you (8) ______________ in every day.

Listening

1.07 **Look at the assignment given to students in their *Introduction to game theory* course. Listen and list the examples given for some of these game theories.**

Assignment: Find a simple scenario or type of game that illustrates one of the following concepts in game theory:

- The zero-sum game—*Rock, Paper, Scissors game*
- The ultimatum
- The assurance situation
- The anti-coordination situation
- The Prisoner's Dilemma

ACADEMIC KEYWORDS

cite	(v)	/saɪt/
prove	(v)	/pruv/
resolution	(n)	/ˌrezəˈluʃ(ə)n/

Critical thinking skill

SELECTING INFORMATION FOR NOTES AND SUMMARIES

When you are listening to a long lecture or discussion, it is not possible to write everything a speaker says, so it is helpful to take notes that record the main points of an argument or explanation. Producing a summary from your notes can help you recall the main points, and decide what is the most important and relevant information. Your notes may look like this:

The point/topic/title

Zero-sum game—e.g., Rock, Paper, Scissors

The most important and relevant information, plus examples

One winner and one loser—always

Trade and economics example: two companies bidding on one contract. Only one company can win, the other has to lose.

The source of the information

Mathematician John von Neumann—academic paper, The Theory of Parlor Games, 1928

1 1.07 **Read the summaries of two concepts in game theory below, and indicate whether they are from the assurance situation (*A*) or the ultimatum (*U*). Listen again to check.**

THE POINT/TOPIC/TITLE

1 The Stag Hunt ___

2 It's a money-sharing situation. ___

THE MOST IMPORTANT AND RELEVANT INFORMATION, PLUS EXAMPLES

3 If the second player refuses the first player's proposal, neither player gets any money. ___

4 There are two outcomes. Either both hunters hunt the stag together, or both hunters hunt rabbits on their own. ___

5 This situation is about risk and a test of social cooperation. ___

6 One real-life example—bilateral trade negotiations between countries. ___

7 This game represents real-life situations in which people or businesses can cooperate together for greater rewards. ___

8 If the negotiation breaks down because the proposal is considered unfair, then both nations lose the benefits of the trading agreement. ___

THE SOURCE OF THE INFORMATION

9 Jean Jacques Rousseau, book, *A Discourse on Inequality*, 1754. ___

10 Güth, article, "On Ultimatum Bargaining Experiments," 1995. ___

2 1.08 **Listen to presentations of the anti-coordination situation and the Prisoner's Dilemma, and complete the notes.**

The point/topic/title

The anti-coordination situation
The game of chicken / Hawk-dove game

The most important and relevant information, plus examples

The source of the information

The point/topic/title

The Prisoner's Dilemma. A mathematical explanation of why people cooperate

The most important and relevant information, plus examples

The source of the information

Developing critical thinking

1 **Discuss these questions in a group.**

1 Can you think of one other real-life situation for each of the concepts of game theory?

2 How much does the knowledge of game theory help you understand decisions in the following topics? Give reasons and any useful examples or sources.

business economics human relations politics sports

2 **Think about the ideas from *Listening 1* and *Listening 2*, and discuss these questions in a group.**

1 Make a list of games that you played as a child. What lessons or life skills did you learn from them?

2 Key components for a game are goals, rules, challenge, and interaction. How much does this reflect the key components for real life? Give reasons for your answer.

Language development

PREPOSITIONAL VERBS

Prepositional verbs are verbs that are accompanied by prepositions when they have an object, for example: *Let's **look at** motivation.*

The preposition does not change the meaning of the verb, unlike in phrasal verbs (see *Phrasal Verbs* box below).

Verb: *look*

Prepositional verbs: *look at, look under, look through* (verb has same meaning)

Phrasal verbs: *look out, look forward to* (verb has different meaning when together with the preposition)

It is important to know which verbs and prepositions go together (collocate).

The verb and preposition are not normally separated in prepositional verbs, but you can insert an **adverb** to show degree.

*This source **refers mainly to** video games as a learning platform.*

1 **Complete the prepositional verb with the correct preposition.**

1 In this game, you collaborate ______________ other people.
2 The neurotransmitter connected ______________ learning is called dopamine.
3 In a game, you have to complete a number of small tasks, and you are generally rewarded ______________ each.
4 Every time you succeed ______________ doing something in a game, you get a credit.
5 Video games help us focus ______________ what we need to see.
6 One example is two companies bidding ______________ one contract.
7 Each player has to put their hands behind their backs and count ______________ four.
8 If they don't trust each other, they will opt ______________ the less rewarding but more certain choice.

2 **Add the adverbs of degree in the box to these sentences.**

carefully	mainly	only	quickly

1 Skimming refers to glancing through a text to determine its gist or general theme.
2 This refers to how community members make decisions and justify their choices.
3 During this class we will look at one concept of game theory because we won't have time to cover any more.
4 Listen to this explanation.

PHRASAL VERBS

Phrasal verbs (also called *multi-word verbs*) are verbs that join together with one or more particles (prepositions or adverbs). Phrasal verbs are not so common in academic use. Instead, single verbs are preferred for formality.

***keep on** playing = **continue** playing*

***bring up** an issue = **raise** an issue* (**bring** an issue **up**)

***make up** a story = **invent** a story* (**make** a story **up**)

1 **Look at the verbs in bold in each sentence below and decide if they are prepositional verbs or phrasal verbs.**

1 The game **consists of** ten rounds.
2 The moderator **weighs up** academic arguments.
3 What the game teaches you is that if you are not successful at first, don't **give up**.
4 His theory **looks at** randomized trials.
5 He didn't **make** it **up**. He has evidence to prove it's true.
6 Let's **go over** these points again.

2 **Rewrite the sentences in exercise 1 using a single verb synonym in the box to replace the verbs in bold. Try to use context to help you guess the meanings of unknown words.**

constitutes	discuss	evaluates	examines	fabricate	quit

3 **Read the following sentences and decide which verb is more appropriate in each context. Why?**

1 The clause in the contract clearly **lays down** / **stipulates** that it would be beneficial for all parties to remain in agreement.
2 This allows us to **ascertain** / **find out** if the formula is correct.
3 The video game giant is **lining up** / **organizing** a new campaign for their latest release.
4 Our findings **support** / **back up** the hypothesis that this method **steps up** / **increases** the heart rate.
5 My to-do list is three pages long! It's going to take forever to **complete** / **get through** everything for the game report.
6 Experts in the field have discovered how to **manage** / **deal with** such occurrences.
7 You know, she really needs to **step up** / **intensify** her training if she wants to **take part** / **participate** in the tournament next month.

SPEAKING Formulating a debate on banning violent electronic games

You are going to practice identifying the linking /r/ sound in order to recognize word boundaries more clearly. You will also learn how to agree and disagree politely. Then you are going to use these skills to participate in a class debate about the effects of violent video and computer games.

Pronunciation skill

IDENTIFYING THE LINKING /r/

Most American, Scottish, and Irish accents can be described as "rhotic" (/ˈroʊtɪk/). This means that when the /r/ sound appears after a vowel sound it is strongly pronounced. When the /r/ sound occurs **between** two vowel sounds it is pronounced even in non-rhotic accents. This is known as the linking /r/.

*Mo**re i**mportantly, each prisoner knows that the other has the same choice.*

*Especially when the consequences a**re i**n the distant future.*

Being able to identify the linking /r/ sound can help you recognize word boundaries, and fine-tune your listening skills.

1 **Look at these sentences from the listenings and underline where the linking /r/ is pronounced.**

1 I'm principally a lecturer at the university's Entertainment Technology Centre.
2 He pinpoints video games as an area that gives us greater insight into how learning takes place.
3 ... no one can learn unless they are able to connect consequences to actions, especially when the consequences are in the distant future.
4 In real life there are, I read anyway, that there are few real zero-sum games.
5 There are two outcomes to the stag hunt. Either both hunters hunt the stag together, or both hunters hunt rabbits on their own.
6 Two drivers drive towards each other on a collision course.

2 1.09 **Listen and check your answers. Practice saying the sentences aloud.**

Speaking skill

AGREEING AND DISAGREEING—DEGREES OF FORMALITY

In an academic situation such as a debate, discussion, or seminar, it is normal for people to agree and disagree with each other. While you may want to make your position clear, it is important to know how to agree and disagree appropriately.

Agreeing

I agree with you 100%. *I'm with you on that one.*
I couldn't agree more. *I am of the same opinion.*

Politeness is more important when expressing disagreement. Purely *No* or *I don't agree* can sound rather abrupt in English. We can soften our disagreement with a lead-in phrase such as *I'm afraid, ...* or *I'm sorry, but ...*

Disagreeing

I'm not so sure about that. *I have to side with (name) on this one.*
I can't agree with you. *I beg to differ.*

1 1.10 **Listen to two dialogues in which two students discuss video games and game theory. Indicate if the students agree (✓) or disagree (✗) with the following statements.**

Statement	Student 1	Student 2
We can become better drivers by playing video games.		
Gaming can improve your creativity.		
It's better to cooperate in the Prisoner's Dilemma situation.		
The best outcome is only possible if you don't cooperate.		

2 **Which dialogue is a formal debate and which is an informal conversation?**

3 **Work with a partner to discuss the statements below. Use the phrases in the *Agreeing and disagreeing—degrees of formality* box to agree and disagree with each other. Explain your reasons.**

- Television news programs give biased reports of the news.
- Health care and education should be free for everyone.
- The popularity of the English language is dangerous for other languages.
- Young people give too much importance to their image.

SPEAKING TASK

BRAINSTORM

Work in groups of three or four. Read the statement below and discuss the assumptions behind the statistics.

> *A study reported that 60% of school boys who played at least one violent video game have admitted to acting aggressively toward someone in real life, compared to 39% of boys who did not play violent games.*

PLAN

You are going to participate in a class debate discussing the following statement:

"All violent electronic games should be banned and removed from the market immediately."

Form three groups.

Group 1: You agree with the statement.

Group 2: You disagree with the statement.

Group 3: You are the moderators of the discussion. This requires you to provide opportunities for balanced discussion, stop any irrelevant or overly long turns, and encourage quieter members to speak out during the discussion.

Group 3 needs to set a time allowance in advance for each group to present their arguments.

Groups 1 and 2 prepare arguments. Think about:

- Dividing your argument between the speakers of your group.
- The level of directness of the language you want to use.
- Replacing phrasal verbs with single verb synonyms.

Group 3 prepares a checklist to evaluate the arguments. Use the checklist below, and add three more items to check.

		Comments or examples:
Is this argument well structured?	Y/N	
Did the speakers provide supporting examples, reasons, and evidence?	Y/N	
Did the speakers summarize each point clearly?	Y/N	
	Y/N	
	Y/N	
	Y/N	

SPEAK

Hold the class debate.

Group 3: Introduce the debate.

Groups 1 and 2: Take turns presenting arguments for and against the statement. As you listen, write down the other group's main arguments.

After each group has presented their arguments, look at your notes. How could you argue against the other group's main argument?

SHARE

At the end of the debate, group 3 decides which group made the best argument. Give feedback on the arguments presented by groups 1 and 2. Which arguments were the most convincing? Why?

Why develop critical thinking skills?

by Stella Cottrell

Benefits of critical thinking skills

Good critical thinking skills bring numerous benefits such as:

- improved attention and observation;
- more focused reading;
- improved ability to identify the key points in a text or other message rather than becoming distracted by less important material;
- improved ability to respond to the appropriate points in a message;
- knowledge of how to get your own point across more easily;
- skills of analysis that you can choose to apply in a variety of situations.

Benefits in professional and everyday life

Skills in critical thinking bring precision to the way you think and work. You will find that practice in critical thinking helps you to be more accurate and specific in noting what is relevant and what is not. The skills listed above are useful to problem-solving and to project management, bringing greater precision and accuracy to different parts of a task.

Although critical thinking can seem like a slow process because it is precise, once you have acquired good skills, they save you time because you learn to identify the most relevant information more quickly and accurately.

Ancillary skills

Critical thinking involves the development of a range of ancillary skills such as:

- observation
- reasoning
- decision-making
- analysis
- judgement
- persuasion.

Realistic self-appraisal

It is likely that you already possess some or all of these skills in order to cope with everyday life, work or previous study. However, the more advanced the level of study or the professional area, the more refined these skills need to be. The better these skills are, the more able you are to take on complex problems and projects with confidence of a successful outcome.

It is likely that many people over-estimate the quality of the critical thinking they bring to activities such as reading, watching television, using the Internet, or to work and study. It is not unusual to assume our point of view is well founded, that we know best, and that we are logical and reasonable. Other people observing us may not share this view. A lack of self-awareness and weak reasoning skills can result in unsatisfactory appraisals at work or poor marks for academic work. Certainly, comments from lecturers indicate that many students are prevented from gaining better marks because their work lacks evidence of rigorous critical thinking.

Nostalgia

CRITICAL THINKING	Organizing qualitative data
	Representative samples
LANGUAGE DEVELOPMENT	Approximation Particulizer and exclusive adverbs
PRONUNCIATION	Juncture
SPEAKING	Identifying sources of information

Discussion point

Discuss these questions with a partner.

1 What would you miss most about your life at home now if you moved to another country? What wouldn't you miss? Make a list of three things you'd miss and three things you wouldn't miss. Compare with your partner.

2 What childhood memories do you associate with the following things?

a game | summer holidays | your bedroom | your best friend | your biggest fear | your school

3 Have you ever felt homesick? When? Where were you?

Vocabulary preview

1 **Read the sentences below and explain the meaning of each of the words or phrases in bold. If you don't know the meaning, try to use context to help you guess. Then check in a dictionary.**

1 I can't **recall** a time when I wasn't trying to create something.
2 I'm really sorry. It must have **slipped my mind**—I really should try to write things down in future.
3 I keep getting **flashbacks** to that terrible day.
4 You really have to **put it behind you** and start to think positively.
5 It was a smell that **evoked** pleasant memories for her.
6 Look at these pictures and tell me if any of them **trigger** any unpleasant memories from your childhood.
7 I'm going to give you some details to **jog your memory**.
8 Do you ever sit back and **reminisce** about those long, hot summers?

2 **Organize the words and phrases into the categories below.**

Remember	Forget

3 **Which of the expressions in exercise 1 are usually used in a negative context? (cf. p. 52—*Connotation*)**

LISTENING 1 How to deal with homesickness

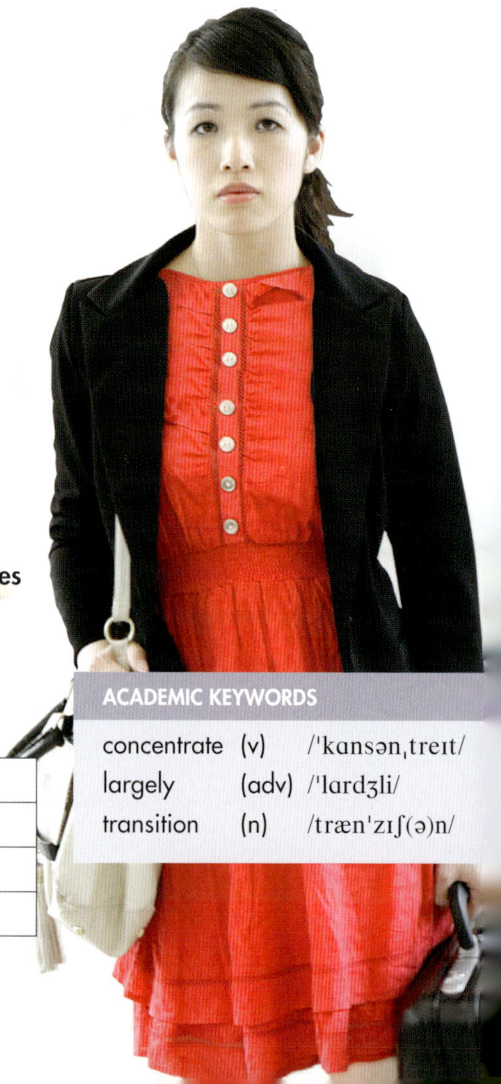

Before you listen

Work with a partner and look at the following remedies for homesickness. Rank each one on the following scale: 1 = not effective at all; 2 = not very effective; 3 = quite effective; 4 = very effective.

a Take something from home with you. ___
b Look at pictures of home. ___
c Join a club. ___
d Use a social network. ___
e Make new friends. ___
f Keep in touch with family back home. ___
g Keep busy. ___
h Talk to somebody. ___

Listening

1 1.11 **Listen to a podcast in which three students share their experiences of homesickness. Match each speaker, Nicola (*N*), Amanda (*A*), and Chloe (*C*) with two homesickness remedies from *Before you listen*.**

2 1.11 **Listen to the three students again and take notes about their original feelings when they arrived, and how they felt afterwards.**

Student	Feel when first arrived?	Feel afterwards?
Nicola		
Amanda		
Chloe		

ACADEMIC KEYWORDS

concentrate	(v)	/ˈkɑnsənˌtreɪt/
largely	(adv)	/ˈlɑrdʒli/
transition	(n)	/trænˈzɪʃ(ə)n/

Critical thinking skill

ORGANIZING QUALITATIVE DATA

Qualitative research aims to answer the questions *why?* and *how?* Unlike quantitative research, its results are not as easily measurable as numeric data.

Qualitative data consists of words rather than numbers; for example, a list of responses given to an open-ended question.

In order to begin analyzing qualitative data, it is useful to organize it by grouping individual items into categories.

For example, participants in a study were asked, "How did you feel on your first day at school?" The raw data (information that has not been examined or organized) for the responses is:

I was really excited. *Terrified.* *I was sad that I wouldn't see my parents.*
I couldn't wait to start! *It wasn't a big deal for me.* *A little bit sad, but also quite excited.*
I was scared of my teacher. *I cried all day.* *I was really nervous.*
Happy and scared at the same time.

Although all these responses are different, they can be grouped into five different categories: sad, excited/happy, scared, mixed feelings, indifferent

Categorizing makes it much easier to draw meaningful conclusions from large amounts of qualitative data.

1 The raw data below is from the focus group that Nicola, Amanda, and Chloe participated in. It lists their responses to the question, "How did homesickness affect you?"

There are some errors in the data. Cross out the two items that are causes of homesickness rather than effects.

depression   different lifestyle, people, & weather   difficulty concentrating
failed exams   felt anxious & insecure   forgetfulness   headaches & dizziness
language barriers   loss of appetite   lost confidence   lost interest in course
missed lectures   neglected research assignments   scored low grades
sleeping problems   stopped going to clubs

2 Work with a partner. Complete the table to organize the responses into four categories.

1 Suffered physical symptoms	2 Suffered psychological symptoms	3 Studies were affected	4 Social life was affected
loss of appetite	*felt anxious & insecure* ________ *difficulty concentrating* *forgetfulness* ________		

3 1.12 Listen to an extract from the podcast in exercise 2 and note which categories in the table above apply to each of the speakers. Write the numbers.

Nicola ______ Amanda ______ Chloe ______

Listening skills

Developing critical thinking

Discuss these questions in a group.

1 Think back to your original views on the most effective remedies for homesickness from the *Before you listen* section. How much have your original views changed? Why?

2 Make two lists, one list with the positive aspects of moving away from home, and the other with the negative aspects. Compare and exchange your ideas. Which list is longer?

3 Do you think it is helpful to talk about personal problems publicly, like Chloe, Amanda, and Nicola did in the podcast? Why or why not?

LISTENING 2 Memory and smell

Before you listen

1 **A survey of some 300 people revealed what were considered to be favorite smells. Add three more of your own favorites to the list. Rank them in order from your most favorite (*1*) to your least favorite (*10*).**

- Freshly ground coffee ___
- Clean sheets ___
- Freshly baked bread ___
- Leather ___
- Fresh flowers ___
- The sea ___
- A new book ___
- ________ ___
- ________ ___
- ________ ___

2 **Compare your list with a partner. Why are these smells pleasant or unpleasant for you?**

ACADEMIC KEYWORDS		
expose	(v)	/ɪk'spoʊz/
express	(v)	/ɪk'spres/
relate	(v)	/rɪ'leɪt/

Listening

1.13 **Listen to a lecture on memory and smell. Take notes using the mind map as a guide.**

Critical thinking skill

REPRESENTATIVE SAMPLES

In academic research, a sample is a group of people used to get information, often to test a theory. The sample represents a much wider group of people, which can be very large and general (the whole human population, or the population of a country) or smaller and more specific (for example, male homeowners aged 26–35 in Mexico City). Since researchers cannot test their theories on everyone in the target group, they use a sample to represent this group as closely as possible. Therefore it is important for the sample to be representative.

Representative means that the characteristics of the sample match the characteristics of the larger group as closely as possible. So for example, if 20–29-year-olds make up 20% of a country's population, but 70% of a sample, then that sample is not representative of the country's population.

Of course, a sample can never be completely representative, but researchers will usually try to ensure that key demographic characteristics such as age, gender, and ethnicity are representative. Depending on the aims of the research, other characteristics such as education level or medical history might also be important.

1 1.14 **Listen to some information about studies by Willander and Toffolo *et al.* Make notes in the table below to answer the questions.**

	Willander	**Toffolo *et al***
1 Was the study representative of the whole human population?		
2 In what way(s) was the study *not* representative of the whole human population?		*All female* *All healthy*
3 Was there a reason the researchers chose to focus on a specific group? (reasons may be inferred from the lecture)	*Participants' childhood was a long time ago—better test of how powerful the memory prompts are*	

2 **If you were conducting a study similar to Willander's, what characteristics would you take into account to make sure your sample was representative? Work with a partner and make a list.**

Developing critical thinking

1 **Discuss these questions in a group.**

1. Think of a smell that evokes a pleasant memory for you, and another that evokes an unpleasant one. Explain the reasons to your group. Are their experiences of these smells similar or different?
2. Were you convinced by the evidence presented in the lecture and the speaker's conclusion? Why or why not?

2 **Think about the ideas from *Listening 1* and *Listening 2*, and discuss these questions in a group.**

1. "The Greek word for 'return' is nostos. Algos means 'suffering.' So nostalgia is the suffering caused by an unappeased yearning to return."
   Milan Kundera
   Do you agree with the above statement that nostalgia is negative? Why? What are the positive sides to nostalgia?
2. In what ways is nostalgia an important feature in your life?

Language development

APPROXIMATION

When you make a reference to a quantity, you can use approximating adverb phrases rather than an exact number. For example:

... ***a little over*** *90% of first-year students at this university experience some level of homesickness.* The example means more than 90%.

You can also use approximation adverb phrases with quantities to express:

Approximately	*somewhere in the region of, around*
More than	*upwards of, (just) over*
Less than*	*under, nearly, almost*
Less than, but also including	*up to*

*Speakers often use *under / less than* to imply that a number is small, or *nearly/almost* to imply that it is large.

Less than *50% of students said they had suffered from homesickness, so it's not a major problem at this university.*

Nearly *50% of students said they had suffered from homesickness, so this is a cause for concern.*

1 Complete the approximating adverb phrases below using the words in the box.

about   like   of   over   so   to

1 The statistics for females in the 15 to 20 age group addicted to video games is **round** ______________ 20%.
2 This method of treating the illness has been around for **a little** ______________ five thousand years.
3 Scientists believe that you can hold **up** ______________ seven items in your short-term memory for between 20 and 30 seconds.
4 It has been by far the most important publication on the topic for **something** ______________ one hundred years.
5 I didn't complete my PhD till I was 30 **or** ______________.
6 The event raised **just short** ______________ a million dollars for the new hospital.

2 Organize the phrases in exercise 1 into the following categories:

Approximately   Less than   Less than, but also including   More than

3 Rephrase the following using an approximation phrase from exercise 1 or the *Approximation* box. Use a different phrase for each sentence.

1 Maximum 50 students per course.
2 9.92 seconds
3 101 scientific papers
4 I completed the test in 26 minutes.
5 Zara scored 89% on the test. She's very smart!
6 The university is relatively new; it was built 19 years ago.

PARTICULIZER AND EXCLUSIVE ADVERBS

We use particulizer and exclusive adverbs to give more information about a verb.

Form	Example
Particulizer adverbs suggest that something is true in most cases, but not always. *largely, particularly, especially, mostly, mainly, predominantly, primarily*	*Homesickness **largely** strikes within the first few days.*
Exclusive adverbs suggest absolute statements that exclude all other possibilities. *precisely, just, solely, only*	*I didn't call home every day. I **only** called home when something new happened.*

Circle the correct adverb to complete each sentence.

1 One of the cases I am **particularly** / **precisely** interested in is that of physical symptoms.
2 The hypothesis that homesickness is **especially** / **solely** psychological does not concur with scientific evidence. There are other factors to consider.
3 It is **particularly** / **precisely** this point, and no other, which proves beyond any doubt that further research is necessary.
4 The warning signs are **especially** / **only** apparent in the first few weeks although there are cases when they appear much later.
5 **Mostly** / **Solely** it is the loss of people, but it can also include routines.
6 **Mostly** / **Only** when the sufferer realizes he is ill, can we start treatment. The realization is the necessary factor.

SPEAKING Conducting a survey on memory

You are going to practice identifying juncture, which is a feature of connected speech, in order to recognize word boundaries more clearly. You will also learn how to identify and provide sources of information. Then you are going to use these skills to conduct a survey on memory.

Pronunciation skill

JUNCTURE

Juncture is a feature of connected speech in English. Final consonant sounds are linked to the following initial vowel sounds, and final vowel sounds are linked to initial consonant sounds.

The reason is the olfactory bulb, which is a part of the brain responsible for the perception of odours.

Smells often call up memories from early times in our lives.

1.15 **Look at the following sentences. Mark the places where juncture takes place. Then listen to each sentence and check your answers.**

1 The student longs for and becomes distressed over the loss of what is familiar and secure.
2 According to the Office of National Statistics, one in five students drop out after the first year of study.
3 When I came last year it was the first time I'd ever been to the U.K.
4 What I would advise is to get out there and make contact with the people around you.
5 In fact, I looked at photos from when I was in Australia.
6 In an experiment aiming to investigate aversive memories, similar to those experienced by PTSD patients, ...

Speaking skill

IDENTIFYING SOURCES OF INFORMATION

When presenting information or evidence in an academic context, speakers should always indicate where it came from—its source. Authentic, reliable, and respected sources are essential in order to support academic arguments (cf. p. 59).

In order to evaluate the relevance of information, it is useful to identify whether the source is a primary or a secondary source. **Primary sources** provide original information, and include raw data from experiments and questionnaires, testimony from witnesses, and documents that were written at the time of the study. **Secondary sources** are edited versions of primary sources and include textbooks, magazine articles, and journal articles which interpret previous findings.

Sometimes the source of information may be a commonly believed fact, or a popular opinion.

Work with a partner. Where do you think you would find the following extracts? What clues do you use to determine your answers? As you consider, note whether source information may have come from a primary source (*P*), a secondary source (*S*), or a popular opinion (*O*).

1 From the aroma of school dinners to the pungent smell of the janitor's disinfectant, nothing transports people back to their childhood more than an unexpected smell. ___
2 Now scientists think they have discovered how scents from the past make such a lasting impression. ___
3 While our other senses may also act as capable cues to forgotten memories, our sense of smell seems to be associated with particularly fast involuntary recall. (Miles & Jenkins, 2000) ___
4 As you can see from the chart, 75% of respondents to my questionnaire were able to identify a particular smell they closely associated with an important event. ___
5 I'd like to make one final point before I go. Now one thing we can say about the memory is that it is usually emotionally laden. You never smell something and remember a page of text, an equation, or a phone number—it is always something emotional, like your first day at school or something similar. ___

SPEAKING TASK

BRAINSTORM

You have been asked to conduct a survey on memory. With a partner, choose one of the titles for a survey below, discussing the reasons for your choice. Think about why you would like to choose the topic. What would you like to learn from the survey?

- Memorable learning experiences
- Short-term memory vs. long-term memory
- Childhood memories
- Sight, smell, taste, touch, sound, and memory
- Memorization techniques

PLAN

1 Together, list the information you want to learn from your survey in the left-hand column of the chart. Write questions that will allow you to obtain the best information you require for each objective. Think about which question types will get the best information:

- *yes/no* questions
- ranking (e.g., order from 1–5)
- multiple choice (e.g., choose a, b, c, or d)

Example:

Objective(s)	Question(s)	Question type
Find out whether food, chemical, or natural smells have the strongest association with childhood.	*Which of the following smells do you associate most strongly with your childhood?* *a) cooking/baking* *b) grass/flowers* *c) disinfectant/chlorine*	*Multiple choice*

2 Decide how many people you need to interview for your survey.

SPEAK

Conduct the interviews with class members and record the responses.

Discuss your findings and draw conclusions. Don't forget to use approximating adverb phrases. How reliable are your conclusions? Is your information reflecting primary sources or secondary sources?

Possible survey reporting format:

- **Purpose:**
  The purpose of our survey was …
- **Methodology:**
  We interviewed X number of people. Out of this number …
- **Findings:**
  We found that …
- **Conclusions:**
  The data demonstrates that …

SHARE

Present your results and conclusions to another pair. If you have access to a computer, present your survey using PowerPoint. Ask your audience if they agree about the accuracy of the survey and if there is anything they would have added to the survey.

Study skills

STUDY SKILLS Listening to extended lectures

Getting started

Discuss these questions with a partner.

1 What difficulties do you have when listening to native speakers?
2 What activities have you done in class to help improve your listening comprehension?
3 What things should you write in your notebook when listening to a university lecture?

Scenario

Read about Imran's experience of attending university lectures in a new country. Think about what Imran could do to overcome his initial problems.

Imran has just started a university degree course in Ireland. He always attained good grades in his English exams and is a confident English speaker. However, he has problems understanding his new lecturers' accents, as he never had native speaker teachers back home. Furthermore, they tend to speak so fast that he is not sure whether he can hear several words or just one.

In his preparatory course for university, his teachers always guided him and helped him to take notes. In spite of this valuable training, Imran finds it difficult to distinguish clear points in his lectures and cannot take effective notes. His new lecturers move from one point to the next very quickly, giving him little indication of what he should write down.

He has also found that there is more to following a lecture than just listening and writing. The lecturers' gestures are important, they use slides to demonstrate points, there are several handouts to read, and the lecturers write on the board while they are talking. Prioritizing what he should be doing at certain moments in the lecture is very challenging for him.

Consider it

Look at these tips on how to overcome problems when listening to lectures. Do you do any of these things?

1 Read the textbook chapter on the topic before the lecture, and think about questions the lecturer may answer.
2 Ask if you can record the lecture to listen to afterwards.
3 Try to take notes on key points like names, dates, and statistics.
4 Make lists and draw diagrams. You can add information after the lecture.
5 When in doubt, always write what you think you hear. Read it aloud in context afterwards to check that it makes sense. For example, "festival" could be misheard as "first of all."
6 Talk to other students as they may be having the same problems as you. Try to exchange techniques on how to overcome your problems.
7 Use abbreviations every time a key word is mentioned rather than repeating the word over and over again. For example, *post-traumatic stress disorder* can be *PTSD*.

Over to you

Discuss these questions with a partner.

1 Which of the *Consider it* tips would be the most effective in helping Imran? Give reasons for your answers.
2 Which tips would be useful for you to try?
3 What other tips or techniques do you have for taking more effective notes or for understanding native speakers?

Risk

CRITICAL THINKING	Using illustrative examples to support an argument Anticipating a conclusion based on reasons and evidence
LANGUAGE DEVELOPMENT	Nominalization Possible, probable, and hypothetical future predictions
PRONUNCIATION	Word stress in word families
SPEAKING	Managing conversation

Discussion point

Discuss these questions with a partner.

1 A dictionary definition of a risk-taker is "someone who risks loss or injury in the hope of gain or excitement." Do you know anyone who is a risk-taker? What kinds of risk do they take?

2 Why do you think people do things that they know are dangerous? Think of three possible reasons.

3 What do you think makes some people take bigger risks than others?

Listening skills

Vocabulary preview

1 Choose the correct word to complete the sentences.

1 The number of *fatals* / *fatalities* makes rock climbing a dangerous pursuit.
2 If you get held up, you ***have*** / ***run*** **the risk** of missing your flight.
3 If you ***take*** / ***get*** **the risk** of investing your money, you could make a lot more.
4 The scaffolding ***poses*** / ***establishes*** **a** real **risk** to passers-by.
5 To work at such great heights, you need **nerves of** ***iron*** / ***steel***.
6 In some parts of the world, the construction industry is an ***unregulated*** / ***unruled*** sector.
7 This man had ***fronted*** / ***faced*** **danger** without fear.
8 I think it's **safe to** ***state*** / ***say*** you've passed the course.
9 The ***odds*** / ***evens*** of a lightning strike are about one in a million.
10 Being bitten is an ***in-*** / ***on*-the-job** danger for any veterinarian.

2 Choose three of the expressions in bold in exercise 1. Create other meaningful sentences for each one.

3 Read the following sentences and correct the grammatical error in each. What rule can you make about the word "risk"?

1 Smokers have a high risk to get cancer.
2 If you eat too much, you run the risk to have health problems.
3 If you don't lock up your bicycle, you risk to lose it.

LISTENING 1 The world's most dangerous jobs

Before you listen

Work with a partner. Make a list of the six most unusual or interesting jobs you can think of in English. Then rank the jobs according to the following criteria.

- most/least fun
- jobs your parents would/wouldn't approve of
- best/worst paid
- most/least dangerous

Listening

1 Look at the jobs in the box below. Which ones do you think would make it onto a list of the world's most dangerous jobs?

bodyguard circus acrobat construction worker fisherman
logger pilot prison warden stunt person window cleaner

2 1.16 Listen to an interview with Dr. Michael White, an expert on dangerous jobs, and check your answer to exercise 1.

ACADEMIC KEYWORDS

average	(adj)	/ˈæv(ə)rɪdʒ/
considerably	(adv)	/kənˈsɪd(ə)rəbli/
leading	(adj)	/ˈlidɪŋ/

Critical thinking skill

USING ILLUSTRATIVE EXAMPLES TO SUPPORT AN ARGUMENT

When presenting an argument, illustrative (= like a real scene) examples make the points clearer and more persuasive.

For example, the argument *Working on a construction site is dangerous* can be made stronger and supported by vivid illustrative examples of the danger, as shown in bold below.

Working on a construction site is dangerous. ***Being crushed by heavy equipment*** *or* ***falling from a great height*** *are on-the-job dangers that many construction workers face every single day.*

1.16 Listen again. Read the examples that support the assertion that certain jobs are dangerous and write the job(s) in the space. Can you think of another example of why these jobs are dangerous?

1 Surfaces slippery with soapy water ______
2 Being hit by ice cold waves, wind, and heavy rain ______
3 Unstable, uneven terrain, such as mountain slopes ______
4 A tree rolling violently down a slope ______
5 Hauling nets or cages that weigh hundreds of pounds ______
6 Working at great heights with chain saws ______
7 High winds striking you ______
8 The momentum and massive weight of a huge branch ______

Developing critical thinking

Discuss these questions in a group.

1 Would you ever consider doing any of these jobs?
2 Choose one of the jobs that you would consider doing. What are the benefits? Do you think these outweigh the risks? Why or why not?
3 Many of the risks connected to these jobs could be prevented with appropriate safety measures. What safety measures are needed, for example, for a stunt person or a construction worker?
4 Is health and safety an important concern for dangerous activities in your country compared to other countries that you know about?

LISTENING 2 What is acceptable risk?

Before you listen

1 Work with a partner. You have been asked to complete this questionnaire as part of a research project. Which one of you is more willing to take risks?

RISK QUESTIONNAIRE

Are you a risk-taker, or are you more cautious by nature? Please answer the questions in this risk survey to help psychology students with their research.

1 Would you buy a car or motorcycle on the Internet? YES / NO

2 Would you do a parachute jump if someone paid you to do it? YES / NO

3 Would you go to work in a foreign country on your own? YES / NO

4 Would you invest a large sum of money in a new business? YES / NO

5 Would you leave your bike unlocked in a public parking lot if you were going to be away for a short period of time? YES / NO

6 Would you download and open a file from the Internet without checking it for viruses first? YES / NO

2 What do you think "acceptable risk" means? Create a definition.

Listening

1 1.17 **Listen to a seminar about acceptable risk. Is your definition from the previous exercise the same? What is the professor's purpose in the seminar?**

1 to **explain** the concept of acceptable risk
2 to **convince** us to take more risks
3 to **criticize** the concept of acceptable risk

2 1.17 **Listen again and decide if the sentences below are true, false, or not given.**

1 Climbing a mountain is as risky as driving a car. ____
2 There are never situations in which there is zero risk. ____
3 An acceptable risk is one that is unlikely to produce a negative result. ____
4 You can never be completely free from danger. ____
5 Environmental health and safety experts like to give measurements about acceptable risk. ____
6 A one-in-a-million chance of death is an acceptable risk. ____
7 Most drinking water in cities has a one-in-a-million chance of causing serious harm. ____
8 If we have no control over the amount of risk we are going to take, then it becomes less acceptable. ____

ACADEMIC KEYWORDS

acceptable	(adj)	/ək'septəb(ə)l/
definition	(n)	/ˌdefə'nɪʃ(ə)n/
point	(n)	/pɔɪnt/

Critical thinking skill

ANTICIPATING A CONCLUSION BASED ON REASONS AND EVIDENCE

In extended lectures, the speaker will often hint at his/her conclusion near the beginning of the lecture, then present reasons and evidence as part of his/her explanation or argument. Finally, he/she will sum up and explicitly state the conclusion at the end.

By identifying reasons and evidence that support the explanation or argument, you can anticipate the conclusion of the lecture before it comes to an end.

1 In the seminar so far, the professor hasn't reached her final conclusion. Choose which of the three paragraphs below would make the most appropriate conclusion.

1 At the end of the day, while mountain climbing and driving a car are both risky activities, you are probably better off getting behind the wheel than going up Everest. Unless you are properly prepared, of course.

2 In the end, we still come back to the notion that danger exists everywhere. There is nothing in life that is completely risk-free. We just have to learn how to manage it, and live with it.

3 To conclude, we've seen how difficult it is to determine acceptable risk. The one-in-a-million measurement is simply not clear enough. The term is elusive and misleading. What is urgently needed is a new approach to safety and danger in our modern world, from drinking water to driving cars.

2 1.18 Listen to the end of the professor's seminar and check your answer.

3 1.17 Now listen again to the full lecture and read the sentences below. Check if they are relevant to the conclusion you chose in exercise 1.

1 ☐ Commonplace activities are hazardous; more people die from car accidents than mountain accidents.

2 ☐ Driving a car is easier than climbing a mountain.

3 ☐ Absolute safety is almost impossible to achieve.

4 ☐ The one-in-a-million measurement for acceptable risk comes from the United States.

5 ☐ Acceptable risk informs our decisions.

6 ☐ A lot of people drive.

7 ☐ Feeling in control will help us tolerate higher risk.

Developing critical thinking

1 Discuss these questions in a group.

1 Do you think the one-in-a-million measurement is a good one for acceptable risk? Why or why not?

2 One could say that if people are not aware of the dangers involved, then they are willing to take higher risks. Think of three examples of this.

2 Think about the ideas from *Listening 1* and *Listening 2*, and discuss these questions in a group.

1 Whose responsibility is public safety? Should it be left primarily to individuals to decide? Or is it the responsibility of governments?

2 Can you think of laws or policies in your country that are designed to reduce risk (e.g., it is illegal to drive without a seat belt)? Do you think people should be allowed to take whatever risks they want if they don't affect others? Why or why not?

Language development

Language development

NOMINALIZATION

Many verbs and adjectives in English can be converted into nouns. This process is called nominalization. Nominalization is more frequent in academic English, both written and spoken. It focuses on the concepts rather than the actions or the people involved, and generally makes the tone of writing more abstract and formal.

Suffixes used to create nouns from verbs or adjectives:
-ty, -ity, -ure, -ation, -sion, -cy, -ment, -ing, -ness, -ence

*Because **we realize** that absolute safety is **almost impossible to achieve** ...*

*→ Because **of the realization** that absolute safety is **an almost impossible achievement** ...*

***When they decide** about health and safety, many authorities are reluctant to specify acceptable risk.*

*→ **In decisions** about health and safety, many authorities are reluctant to specify acceptable risk.*

1 **Look at the following nouns from this unit. What adjectives or verbs are they formed from?**

activity danger disappointment drowning
explosion measurement organization safety

2 **Look at the verbs and adjectives in the box. Convert them into nouns using the appropriate suffix.**

achieve decide expand expect generous
insecure involve uncertain

3 **Rewrite the sentences so they mean the same, changing the words in bold to nouns.**

1 The company has **invested** millions of dollars in risk assessment.
The company has made an investment of millions of dollars in risk assessment.

2 The government questions whether this report is **accurate**.

___

3 Do not underestimate how **serious** the problem is.

___

4 If you're a little **intelligent**, most risks can be avoided.

___

5 Our company is **committed** to making the public safe at all times when people are on our trains.

___

6 The president had always known that risks **existed**, but chose to ignore this information.

___

7 The paper **included** reports from several experts, which gave it more authority.

___

POSSIBLE, PROBABLE, AND HYPOTHETICAL FUTURE PREDICTIONS

There are many different ways to express possible, probable, and hypothetical future predictions.

Form	Example
We can use a variety of adverbs, such as *definitely, probably,* and *possibly* to modify predictions.	*There **definitely** won't be any danger of people falling.* *The risk will **probably** be worth it.*
We can also use *It's … that …* with adjectives such as (*highly*) *likely/unlikely, inconceivable,* and *doubtful*.	*It's **highly unlikely** that the structure will collapse.* *It's **inconceivable** that he will lose.*
We can use the following expressions instead of *if* to introduce first conditionals: *providing** (= *provided that*) / *assuming* (*that*) *in the event of* (+ noun) *as long as*	***Providing** you assess the risks, you are complying with H&S guidelines.* ***In the event of** fire, the elevators will not work.* ***As long as** the company informs the public of the risks, they can sell their product.*
The following expressions can be used to introduce first or second conditionals: *even if* *unless* (meaning *if … not*) *suppose/supposing**	***Even if** flying was 100% safe, people would still fear it more than driving.* ***Unless** you are fully aware of the risks, you shouldn't try an extreme sport.* ***Suppose** we uninstalled the firewall? Then could we download those files?*

*Note: *providing* and *supposing* are more common in British English.

1 Complete each sentence below. Which warnings are more likely to be from spoken language? Which are more likely to be from written language? What do they refer to?

1 In the ____________ of a sudden loss of cabin pressure, oxygen masks will be lowered automatically from the panel above your seat.
2 Be careful! If you touch the pan, you will ____________ burn your hand.
3 Your personal data will be safe ____________ you don't reveal your PIN number to anyone.
4 ____________ you take proper safety precautions, rock climbing is a very dangerous sport.
5 ____________ you have anti-virus software, your computer may still be at risk from multiple threats.
6 ____________ it doesn't open when I jump? What then?
7 ____________ the pilot is competent and the aircraft is in good condition, flying is safer than traveling by car.
8 Of course it's dangerous. ____________ you install a gate, the child will fall down the stairs.

2 Complete the advice for students with your own ideas.

A D V I C E for students

- Remember, as long as you ____________, you ____________.
- If you have an exam at the end of the week, you ____________.
- Homework is always ____________, even if ____________.
- Providing you ____________, then you ____________.
- You should always sit ____________, unless ____________.
- You probably won't ____________, unless ____________.

SPEAKING Undertaking an informal risk assessment

You are going to learn about word stress in word families. You will also learn about different ways in which you can manage a conversation. You are then going to use these skills to participate in a conversation in which you undertake an informal risk assessment.

Pronunciation skill

WORD STRESS IN WORD FAMILIES

A word family is a group of words that all have the same root word. In many cases, the stressed syllable doesn't change. For example, in the word family for the root word *risk*, the syllable is stressed in all derivatives of the word.

●	●•	●••	●••
risk	risky	riskily	riskiness

However, in some word families, the word stress changes when the word changes, for example, in the word family for the root word *origin*.

●••	•●••	•●••	•••●••
origin	original	originate	originality

Match the example words in the box below with the rules. Then cross out the incorrect option in bold.

dangerous destruction impossible sunglasses well-behaved

1 In words ending in *-sion*, *-tion*, we often stress the **last** / **the second to last** syllable in the word. ______________
2 Adjective suffixes are usually **stressed** / **unstressed**. ______________
3 Negative prefixes are often **stressed** / **unstressed**. ______________
4 In compound nouns, the stress is on the **first** / **second** syllable. ______________
5 In compound adjectives, the first part is **stressed** / **unstressed**. ______________

Speaking skill

MANAGING CONVERSATION

To take part in a conversation in English you need to be able to follow what is happening and participate. However, to take part more effectively, you also need to be able to get your point across by managing the conversation. Changing the topic, staying on topic, and coming back to an earlier topic are all ways of doing this.

Look at the phrases below. Which ones can be used to change the topic? Which ones can be used to stay on topic? Which ones can be used to come back to a previous topic? Mark the phrases *CT* (change topic), *ST* (stay on topic), or *CB* (come back to previous topic).

1 If I might add something to that … ___
2 If I could move on to the next point … ___
3 Another point on this subject would be … ___
4 Changing the subject completely … ___
5 If I could just go back to what I was saying before … ___
6 Incidentally … ___
7 But, to return to my previous point … ___
8 Sorry, if I could just finish this point. ___
9 That reminds me … ___
10 Just one more thing before we change the subject … ___

SPEAKING TASK

BRAINSTORM

Work in groups of three or four. You are going to undertake an informal risk assessment for a specific work-related situation. Choose one of the company descriptions below, or decide on your own.

1

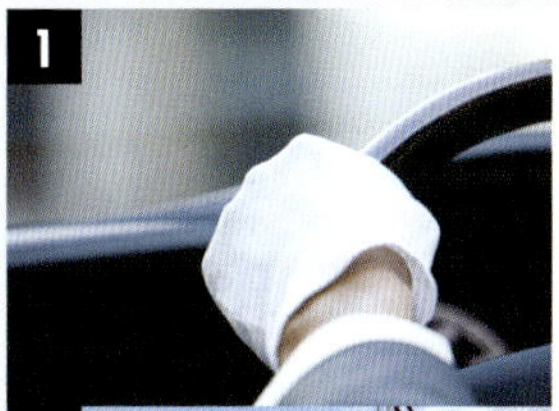

2

3

Cars4U is a driving service that specializes in chauffeur-driven executive cars, couriers, and limousines for special events. All the drivers have at least ten years' driving experience. The cars are maintained and checked once a month and are changed every five years. Each car is equipped with GPS and a car phone. The customers are often very demanding, and sometimes ask the driver to drive fast.

Samson Bros Construction has a contract to build a four-story parking garage. They have 20 builders from several different countries working for them. The parking garage will be situated in the center of town. It is winter and cold weather is expected, with high winds and lots of snow.

English Away is a student travel agency that organizes educational trips to England, Scotland, and Ireland. The trips include flights, hotels, and sightseeing tours. The students that go on these trip are all aged 16 to 24. There is one supervisor.

PLAN

1 **Work individually. Identify all the risks and dangers you can think of in your chosen situation. For each risk, think of an illustrative example to support it. Use the ideas in the box to help you.**

car accidents	communication problems	computer viruses	equipment malfunction
falls	fire	floods	heavy equipment
lawsuits for poor service	theft	weather	

The builders would be using heavy equipment. There is a risk of serious accidents if the equipment malfunctions, or falls from a height, indiscriminately crushing workers below.

2 **Take notes about ways that each risk could be minimized.**

Risk	Action needed to minimize risk
heavy equipment	*check equipment is functioning correctly*
	train staff to use equipment safely

SPEAK

In your groups, discuss your ideas. Make predictions using first and second conditionals, using your notes from the planning stage.

If we train staff to use the equipment safely and check that it is functioning correctly, it's unlikely that there will be any accidents.

Listen to what the other members of your group say, and get your points across by managing the conversation. Identify the three most important risks in your risk assessment and how you propose minimizing these risks.

SHARE

Explain your risk assessment to another group. Can the other group hypothesize about possible failures of your proposals to minimize your risks?

Suppose you don't have enough time or money to provide training for the staff ...

Critical thinking: Knowledge, skills and attitudes

by Stella Cottrell

Interpreting your score

Going through the questionnaire below may raise some questions about what you know or don't know about critical thinking. The lower the score, the more likely you are to need to develop your critical thinking skills. A score over 75 suggests you are very confident about your critical thinking ability. It is worth checking this against objective feedback such as from your tutors or colleagues. If your score is less than 100, there is still room for improvement! If your score is under 45, you may find it helpful to speak to an academic counsellor, your tutor or a supervisor to root out the difficulty.

Self-evaluation

For each of the following statements, rate your responses as outlined below.

5 = 'strongly agree' 4 = 'agree' 3 = 'sort of agree' 2 = 'disagree' 1 = 'strongly disagree'

		Rating 5–1
1	I feel comfortable pointing out potential weaknesses in the work of experts.	
2	I can remain focused on the exact requirements of an activity.	
3	I know the different meanings of the word 'argument' in critical thinking.	
4	I can analyse the structure of an argument.	
5	I can offer criticism without feeling this makes me a bad person.	
6	I am aware of how my current beliefs might prejudice fair consideration of an issue.	
7	I am good at recognising the signals used to indicate stages in an argument.	
8	I find it easy to separate key points from other material.	
9	I am very patient in going over the facts in order to reach an accurate view.	
10	I am good at identifying unfair techniques used to persuade readers.	
11	I find it easy to evaluate the evidence to support a point of view.	
12	I usually pay attention to small details.	
13	I find it easy to weigh up different points of view fairly.	
14	If I am not sure about something, I will research to find out more.	
15	I can present my own arguments clearly.	
16	I understand how to structure an argument.	
17	I can spot inconsistencies in an argument easily.	
18	I am good at identifying patterns.	
19	I am aware of how my own upbringing might prejudice fair consideration of an issue.	
20	I know how to evaluate source materials.	
	Score out of 100	

UNIT 5

Sprawl

CRITICAL THINKING	Recognizing logical order Evaluating against criteria
LANGUAGE DEVELOPMENT	Connotation Academic verbs
PRONUNCIATION	Contrastive stress
SPEAKING	Supporting proposals

Discussion point

Discuss these questions with a partner.

1 What is the most interesting neighborhood you have visited, in your city or another city? How would you describe it? Choose from the adjectives in the box.

affluent	bustling	gloomy	run down	sleepy	trendy	vibrant

2 Think of three ways to improve your neighborhood, for example, creating a new retail area or establishing a speed limit for traffic. Why would you make these changes?

3 Do you live in your capital city? If not, would you like to? Is it a good place to live? Why or why not?

Vocabulary preview

1 **Put the following phrases into the correct category. There are two words for each category.**

drainage system freeway merchant pedestrian streetcar
suburb trolley urban block urban decay urban sprawl

City infrastructure	Urban issues	People in the city	Places in or around the city	City transportation

2 **Complete these definitions with the words from exercise 1.**

1 A ____________ is a wide, fast road in a U.S. city that you do not pay to use.
2 Every city has a ____________. This is a series of pipes and passages that take water or waste liquid from an area.
3 One of the main problems in every city is when areas become run-down and undesirable to live in. This is called ____________.
4 The outward spreading of a city is referred to as ____________. This phrase normally has a negative meaning.
5 A ____________, also known as a ____________, uses electric power from wires hanging above the road.
6 Someone who walks in a town or city is called a ____________.
7 A ____________ is a person who sells goods.
8 An area of buildings surrounded by streets on four sides is called an ____________.
9 A ____________ is a residential area outside a city normally associated with the middle classes.

LISTENING 1 Cars and cities

Before you listen

Look at the ways of getting around a city below. Rank them from best to worst. Consider: speed, price, comfort, convenience.

bicycle bus motorcycle on foot
private car subway taxi trolley

Listening

1.19 **You are going to listen to a university lecture from an urban planning course on cars and cities. Listen and take notes for the following dates:**

pre-1880 1880–1920 post-1920 2011

ACADEMIC KEYWORDS

dominate	(v)	/ˈdɑmɪˌneɪt/
eliminate	(v)	/ɪˈlɪmɪˌneɪt/
gain	(v)	/geɪn/

Critical thinking skill

RECOGNIZING LOGICAL ORDER

In lectures, the speaker should present points in a logical order so that similar points are grouped together. You, the listener, can follow an argument more easily if you can see how each point is connected with the preceding one. Recognizing logical order can help you to anticipate what is coming next, or fill in gaps if there are parts of the lecture you miss.

Anticipating

… it is currently estimated that almost one half of all land in cities is dedicated in one way or another to cars.

We can anticipate that this will be followed by further details about how this land is dedicated to cars.

Streets, roads, parking lots, gas stations, signals, traffic signs, and companies devoted to the automobile industry are such a part of the modern city that we barely notice them.

Filling in gaps

The automobile's impact was ________________. Suddenly people had access, individually, to all kinds of places previously difficult to get to.

We can deduce from the second sentence that the word in the gap should be something meaning "big" or "significant."

1 Look at the statements from the lecture in the table below. Underline the information that should logically follow each statement.

Statement from the lecture	Information that follows
1 The automobile, coupled with the arrival of long distance forms of communication such as the telephone and telegraph, meant that cities could continue to expand and become progressively more decentralized.	**a** The suburbs became pushed out further and further. **b** Billboards were placed along the roads from the city centre to the countryside promoting many products and services.
2 The automobile had transformed the landscape into real estate.	**a** Housing prices rose steadily in this period. **b** Empty land, now connected by roads and cars, could gain value and be sold.
3 The post-automobile city is not car-free, but is redesigned to offer infrastructure for pedestrians and those who desire to live without cars.	**a** This vision of the future gives us a city in which we can walk without the need of transport. **b** There are more parks, gardens, pathways, pedestrian shopping streets, and bicycle lanes.

2 Look at the statements from the lecture in the table below. Deduce the words in the gaps by looking at the information that follows. It does not have to be the exact word used in the lecture, but it should have the same meaning.

Statement from the lecture	Information that follows
1 Cities were small and compact, and they featured a mixture of residences and ________________.	People were expected to walk to work.
2 Governments also began to build freeways and ________________ …	The most famous example of this in American history was the Federal Interstate Highway Act of 1956 …
3 The European Union, in a 2011 White Paper on transportation, revealed that they wanted to ________________ conventionally fuelled ________________ from all cities by 2050.	It is commonly understood that people would have to rely on electric cars, or on public transport.

3 1.19 **Listen to the lecture again and check your answers to exercises 1 and 2.**

Developing critical thinking

Discuss these questions in a group.

1 How often do you travel by car in a city? Why do people who live in cities need cars?

2 In a quality city, a person should be able to live their entire life without a car, and not feel deprived.—Paul Bedford, Professor of City Planning, University of Toronto.

Do you agree with the above statement? What three things would you enjoy about living in a post-automobile city? Why? Give reasons.

3 What incentives or campaigns have there been in your city to encourage people to use public transportation? Have these incentives been successful?

Copenhagen

New Delhi

LISTENING 2 Making cities more liveable

Before you listen

1 Look at the following factors that make a city liveable. Write down which factors you consider important (*I*) or not important (*NI*). Add two more factors that would be important for you.

- Accommodation is reasonably priced. ___
- Has numerous tourist attractions. ___
- Has a large number of parks and green spaces. ___
- Is on the coast. ___
- Has a warm climate all year. ___
- Has an excellent public transportation system. ___
- Has good parking in the city center. ___
- Has cultural events throughout the week. ___
- ______________________ ___/___
- ______________________ ___/___

2 Compare your answers with a partner and explain your reasons.

Listening

You are going to listen to a podcast in which the representatives of two cities discuss the various innovative ideas they have promoted to make their cities more liveable.

1.20 Listen to part 1 and match the criteria of a liveable city with their definitions.

1 *Resilience* refers to ___
2 *Inclusiveness* refers to ___
3 *Authenticity* refers to ___
a the city's capacity to create an integrated society.
b how the city appears to people.
c the city's capacity to change according to what its residents need.

ACADEMIC KEYWORDS

criterion (plural: criteria)	(n)	/kraɪˈtɪriən/
element	(n)	/ˈelɪmənt/
promote	(v)	/prəˈmoʊt/

Critical thinking skill

EVALUATING AGAINST CRITERIA

To evaluate is defined as "to think carefully about something before making a judgement about its value, importance, or quality."* When evaluating something in an academic context, you will usually need to evaluate it against defined criteria. Consider the following example:

To address the city's transportation problems, a new subway system would be a better solution than the creation of new bus routes.

This statement is meaningless if we don't know what criteria are being used to define what is "better." If the main criteria are speed and the reduction of road traffic, for example, then concluding that the subway system is the best solution would be a fair evaluation. However, if the main criteria are minimal cost and minimal construction work, then the creation of new bus routes would actually be a better solution.

*(Source: www.macmillandictionary.com)

1 1.21 **Listen to part 2 about Copenhagen and make notes in the table to evaluate its projects against the criteria below.**

2 2.01 **Listen to part 3 about New Delhi and make notes in the table.**

Criteria	Copenhagen	New Delhi
Resilience: How well do the projects deal with economic and environmental challenges?		
Inclusiveness: How well do the projects include *all* citizens?		
Authenticity: How well do the projects maintain the local character of the city?		

3 **Based on the notes you have made in the table, which city do you think should win the award? Compare your ideas with a partner.**

Developing critical thinking

1 **Discuss these questions in a group.**

1 Think of one other criterion you would use to evaluate the projects for making Copenhagen and New Delhi more liveable. Think about the following areas:

cultural value   financial viability   innovation   social responsibility

2 If you were evaluating the projects based on this criterion, which city do you think would win the award? Discuss with a partner.

2 **Think about the ideas from *Listening 1* and *Listening 2*, and discuss these questions in a group.**

1 Do you think we can learn from the past when we think about how to best organize the way we live in cities? Give reasons.

2 Would the best solution to expanding cities be to start again and build new communities in the future? Why or why not? Give reasons.

Language development

CONNOTATION

Connotation refers to the wide range of positive and negative associations many words carry with them. When a speaker chooses words with strong positive or negative connotations, this is often an indication of his/her opinion on a topic.

*The upper classes began to **flee** the city center to live in newly created suburbs.*

Flee has a similar meaning to *leave*, but it has a stronger negative connotation. The speaker has chosen this word because he sees the situation as negative.

*Another plan is to **rejuvenate** an ancient drainage system.*

Rejuvenate has a similar meaning to *improve*, but it has a stronger positive connotation. The speaker has chosen this word because she believes the plan would be a very positive development.

1 **Look at the words below. Mark each one + (positive connotation), – (negative connotation), or ≈ (neutral). Choose the word in each group that has a different connotation.**

1	cramped ___	populous ___	overcrowded ___
2	reckon ___	contemplate ___	reflect ___
3	growth ___	expansion ___	sprawl ___
4	struggle ___	strive ___	endeavor ___
5	ample ___	enough ___	abundant ___
6	push out ___	expand ___	extend ___

2 **Choose the correct option for each sentence.**

1 I am delighted to accept this great ____________ on behalf of our city.
   a burden   b load   c responsibility

2 This neighborhood offers you the most ____________ housing in the city.
   a exuberant   b refined   c ramshackle

3 I find the Mayor extremely incompetent. He has just ____________ an urban think tank at the last minute.
   a thrown together   b set up   c assembled

4 This elegant twenty-first century urban block ____________ the ancient Ziggurat communities.
   a pays homage to   b poses as   c mimics

5 I am afraid that the dawn of the post-automobile city may mean that many workers in the car industry will have to be ____________.
   a dismissed   b cut out   c laid off

Language development

ACADEMIC VERBS

Certain verbs appear more frequently in academic texts than they do elsewhere. We can call them "academic verbs." They usually have a more specific meaning than "non-academic" verbs.

Examples of academic verbs: *account (for), acquire, assess, constitute, demonstrate, derive, govern, obtain, perceive, specify, yield ...*

There are many groups of academic verbs that have a similar meaning. They may appear to be synonyms, but they differ in specific detail.

(cf. also p. 22 to review the preference of single verbs over phrasal verbs.)

1 The following academic verbs from the listening texts all relate to *change*. Match the words with their dictionary definitions below.

1. There can be few inventions that we know of today that have **transformed** the cities as much as the automobile. ___
2. In Copenhagen we feel that urban planners have to **adapt** to the needs of the people. ___
3. We may be about to **shift** towards a fourth type of city, the post-automobile city. ___
4. We aim to **develop** these canals into public areas, for example, walkways and cycle paths for people to enjoy. ___
5. Our aim is to enhance people's lives by **varying** the type and amount of lighting from the dark autumn months to the longer and darker winter months. ___
6. If we look at the history of urban growth in the United States, we can see that our cities have gradually **evolved** due to the automobile. ___

a consciously change your way of thinking
b make changes in something in order to give more diversity
c make something or someone completely different
d change land for a particular purpose
e progressively change over a period of time
f change your ideas or behavior so that you can deal with a new situation

2 Work with a partner. Take turns testing each other on the meanings of the words in bold in exercise 1.

3 Put an appropriate verb from exercise 1 in the correct form in each of the spaces below.

1. We really need to ______________ our methods of gathering information from the public. We have to appeal to people from all walks of life.
2. In the future, cities will have to ______________ to new challenges.
3. That would be impossible because we have naturally ______________ into an urban society.
4. He is the nation's most celebrated architect because he totally ______________ city centers up and down the country.

Speaking skills

SPEAKING Presenting a proposal of an action plan for an urban issue

You are going to practice expressing opinions in order to put your ideas across with sufficient support and examples. You will also learn how to identify and use contrastive stress. Then you are going to use these skills to present a proposal for an action plan for an urban issue.

Pronunciation skill

CONTRASTIVE STRESS

Stress on certain words in a sentence can be used to indicate contrast between two things or to correct previous information. When you are contrasting two ideas or concepts, the stress should fall on both noun or gerund phrases, to highlight the differences through intonation as well as meaning.

Unlike some liveability ranking data this award doesn't focus on salaries, it focuses on well-being.

While banning cars from our city centers would be one solution, improving cycling facilities would be a more positive step.

1 Predict where the contrastive stress will fall in these sentences.

1. Our current city planning isn't only about architecture; it also includes green spaces.
2. New Delhi isn't India's largest city; it's the largest metropolitan area.
3. If parks are the lungs, then water is the blood of a city!

2 2.02 **Listen and check.**

3 Write three untrue sentences about your partner. Your partner will correct the information using contrastive stress.

Speaking skill

SUPPORTING PROPOSALS

When making proposals or explaining a plan of action, it is important to put your ideas across with sufficient support and examples. Here are some ways to do this effectively.

Supporting your proposal with a reason

I say this because …   Let me explain why / the reasons for …   The reason is … One reason for …

Giving examples

For instance …   For example …   Let me give you a clear example …   As an example …

Referring to generally held beliefs / common sense

These expressions can also be used to restate/reformulate ideas (cf. p. 104).

It's obvious that …   It makes sense to …   As we all know …   Common sense tells us …

1 2.03 **Listen to four extracts. What problems are being discussed? What solutions are proposed?**

2 Propose solutions to these problems with a partner.

- There are too many delegates on the initial conference invitation list.
- You will not be able to finish a report before the deadline.

SPEAKING TASK

BRAINSTORM

You are going to plan and present a proposal for an action plan for an urban-related issue. In a proposal, you identify a problem and state how you will solve that problem.

With a partner, make a list of common urban problems connected to the categories below. Think of reasons for these problems, and provide evidence or examples of how these problems affect city dwellers.

green areas housing pollution population retail areas traffic

PLAN

Choose one of the problems from the brainstorm stage. Plan a proposal to deal with the problem. A proposal format identifies a problem, states the effect of the problem, and then proposes a solution to the problem, with reasons and evidence. A strong proposal is based on factual information rather than opinion.

SPEAK

Find other pairs who chose the same problem as you. Present your proposal to those pairs. Remember to give reasons and evidence. Also remember to support your arguments, using appropriate language. (Don't forget to also try and practice some of the previously-learned skills: stress, intonation, using academic verbs, nominalization, and particulizer and exclusive adverbs.) Listen to the other speakers' proposals, ask questions, and make comments.

SHARE

As a whole class, discuss the various proposed solutions you have heard. Which proposals were presented well and could be made into a campaign video to be forwarded to a relevant group?

Study skills

STUDY SKILLS Recording achievement

Getting started

Discuss these questions with a partner.

1 Think about the last course or module you passed. What did you do to achieve this?
2 What did you learn about yourself from this experience?
3 How can you use this knowledge to help you in the future?

Scenario

Read about what Kyung-mi has been advised to do in order to further her academic progress. What information would you include in a personal portfolio?

Kyung-mi has had a successful first semester academically. She has passed all of her module one exams and is ready to start module two. Her faculty advisor has told her that she must record her achievement and use this knowledge to further her progress.

The faculty advisor has also suggested that she keep a personal portfolio. However, Kyung-mi is not sure how to do this. She has always been a good student and has always passed exams. She puts this down to hard work. She has a record of the units and modules passed, but this does not seem like a personal record.

Her friend has told her that her hard work needs to be defined more clearly and that she should consider goal achievement, personal development, and motivation in order to use this experience to help her in her future academic development. Kyung-mi has also decided to take notes on what she did in order to pass the modules.

Consider it

Look at these tips on how to record achievement. Do you do any of these things?

1 Write about how you managed to achieve your objectives. For instance, the stages you went through or the personal qualities you used.
2 Include the personal goals you have achieved. For example, becoming more confident in your own ability or finding a study partner.
3 Take notes on what you learned about yourself. For example, what time of day is best for studying, where the best place to study is, or how your level of confidence has changed.
4 Record the ways you kept yourself motivated during the process.
5 Make a list of new skills and qualities you have gained and provide examples of them.
6 Prepare yourself to continue your progress. Make a personal statement of new goals and objectives. State their significance both personally and academically. Continue to update your progress—where you are at the present time, where you want to be, and how you will make progress.

Over to you

Discuss these questions with a partner.

1 What tips from *Consider it* would you like to try? Why?
2 Discuss one of your achievements using tips 1–6. How much does this help you understand your success?
3 What tips would you add to the above list?

Legacy

CRITICAL THINKING	Source validity Use of the passive in source citations
LANGUAGE DEVELOPMENT	Inversion Collocations: *way*
PRONUNCIATION	Pausing for dramatic emphasis
SPEAKING	Emphasizing important information—repetition and contrastive pairs

Discussion point

Discuss these questions with a partner.

1 Read the quotations. Do you agree with them? Why or why not? Which one do you prefer and why? Do you have similar quotes in your language?

2 "After ______________, things were never the same again." Think of an invention, a discovery, or a kind of food or drink to complete the sentence. Give reasons for your choice.

3 What qualities does someone or something need to have in order to leave a significant legacy?

"We don't inherit the earth from our ancestors, we borrow it from our children."
Native American proverb

"If you would not be forgotten as soon as you are dead, either write something worth reading or do something worth writing."
Benjamin Franklin

"No legacy is so rich as honesty."
William Shakespeare

Vocabulary preview

1 Circle the two synonyms in each group of words.

1	launch	withdrawal	unveiling
2	to maintain	to revolutionize	to change the face of
3	to overlook	to address	to deal with
4	to hand down	to pass on	to withhold
5	achievement	flop	success
6	to convey	to conceal	to express
7	to stand to	to be likely to	to be unlikely to
8	routine	ritual	custom

2 Work with a partner. Discuss any difference in connotation between the synonyms. More than one answer might be possible.

3 Use the correct form of one of the synonyms in each row from exercise 1 to complete the sentences below.

1 The ______________ of the iPhone changed the way people interact.
2 The Internet has ______________ international communication.
3 The best way to ______________ urban pollution is to ban private cars.
4 The best ideas are ______________ from generation to generation.
5 The true measure of ______________ is not money-related.
6 It is always best to ______________ your ideas as simply as possible.
7 Banks that ______________ make huge profits this year should donate some of the profits to charity.
8 Traditional ______________ are dying out in most countries.

4 Do you agree or disagree with the statements in exercise 3?

LISTENING 1 Family food legacies

Before you listen

Discuss these questions with a partner.

1 How often do you eat with your family?
  a 7 days a week b 4–6 days a week c 0–3 days a week
2 What advantages are there in eating together as a family? Is this common in your culture? Why or why not?
3 Who tends to prepare the meals in your family? Why is this?

Listening

1 2.04 Listen to a lecture on family food legacies. Take notes on the topic using these mind map headings.

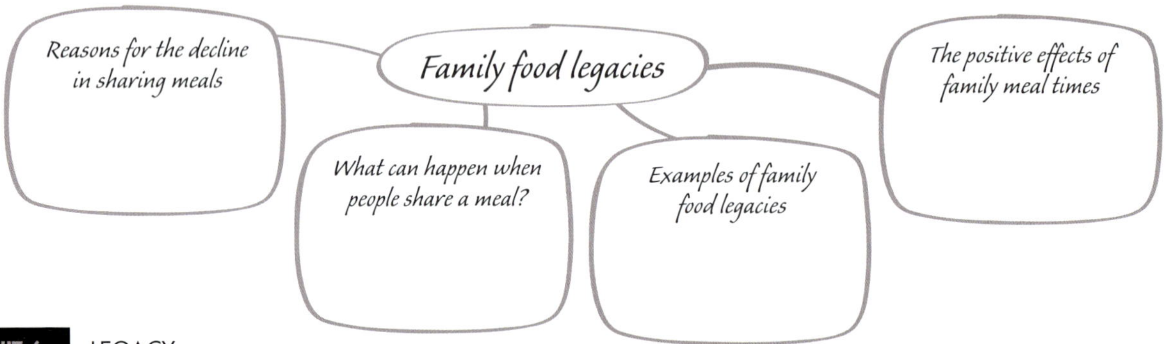

2 **Work with a partner and compare your mind maps. Do you agree with the information the speaker presented in the lecture?**

ACADEMIC KEYWORDS		
analysis	(n)	/əˈnæləsɪs/
examine	(v)	/ɪɡˈzæmɪn/
strengthen	(v)	/ˈstreŋθən/

Critical thinking skill

SOURCE VALIDITY

Remember that it is important to note sources of information (cf. p. 61). Citing sources in your presentation can give you more credibility. Likewise, you may need to critically assess other speakers' sources by asking yourself these questions:

- Does the source material actually exist?
- Does the speaker present the source material accurately?
- Is the citation from an authoritative source or from, e.g., an amateur blogger?
- Is the source material useful for my own research needs?
- Does/Did the source material make a recognized contribution to the area of study?
- Even if a primary source is cited, was the research valid? For example, if the research only used two participants, but makes sweeping statements about its findings, then it might not be valid.

1 2.04 **Listen to the lecture again and complete the table below.**

Information	Source name	Publication name	Primary (P)/ Secondary (S) source?	Authoritative source?	Valid research participant base?
		n/a		*✓ Anthropologist at Rutgers University, U.S.*	
			S		*✓ 182,000 youngsters*
	Russell Belk	*"Sharing," Journal of Consumer Research, UoC*			
Rich and delicious memories connected to eating at home.		*Online forum*			
A ritual makes a family feel united.			*S*		

2 **Which information from the chart in exercise 1 lacks validity? Which has stronger validity? What is missing from information that you would need to follow up? How would you set about following it up?**

Developing critical thinking

Discuss these questions in a group.

1 Is sharing a meal a valuable way of teaching a person to be a member of a culture or society? Why or why not?

2 Why do you think so many of our traditions are centered around meals?

3 Go back to *Speaking skill* exercise 1 on page 54. Rank the extracts from most reliable (*1*) to least reliable (*4*). Give reasons for your choices.

LISTENING 2 Technology legacies

Before you listen

1 Choose one of the items in the box and think about how your life would be different without it. Discuss with a partner.

2 Which of these do you think was the most significant and groundbreaking invention? Do you know who invented any of the items in exercise 1, when they were invented, or from which countries the items originated?

3 Do you recognize any of the people in these pictures?

a

b

c

Listening

2.05 Listen to three students in a seminar discussing key figures in the field of computing. Write the name of the person each student chooses and the reason for their choice.

	Key figure	Reason for choice
Student 1		
Student 2		
Student 3		

ACADEMIC KEYWORDS

contribution (n) /ˌkɑntrɪˈbjuʃ(ə)n/
introduce (v) /ˌɪntrəˈdus/
summarize (v) /ˈsʌməˌraɪz/

Critical thinking skill

USE OF THE PASSIVE IN SOURCE CITATIONS

Passive constructions are often used in formal English. Passive grammar will often be taught at higher level English classes. Using the passive puts the emphasis on what happened rather than on who was involved. The passive uses the verb *be* + the past participle.

It ***is thought*** *that the iPad is one of the most significant technological inventions of late.*

It has ***been stated*** *that Tim Berners-Lee invented the Internet.*

Although the above sentences sound formal, such passive structures can give the false impression that a source is being cited. In the second sentence above, ask yourself, "Who stated that?" We don't know, and we might need to prompt the speaker to give more support to his or her statement.

1 2.05 **Listen to the three speakers again. Identify three citations that use passive constructions in relation to the inventors, and complete the table.**

Inventor	A citation that uses a passive construction
Apple® / Steve Jobs	
Alan Turing	
Tim Berners-Lee	

2 **Re-phrase the citations so that they reference specific sources. For the purpose of this exercise, you can invent some fake sources, but try to make them sound as authentic and authoritative as possible.**

Developing critical thinking

1 **Discuss these questions in a group.**

1 Compare the students' arguments. Did they all provide illustrative examples to support their choices?
2 Make a list of all the technological items you have and what you do with them. What would be the effect if these things didn't exist?

2 **Think about the ideas from *Listening 1* and *Listening 2*, and discuss these questions in a group.**

1 Which legacy do you think has more impact on society—technological change or changes in family structure? Give reasons for your answer.
2 Make a list of the things you and your families do together that involve technology, for example, playing games together or keeping in touch. How much influence does technology have on your family rituals?
3 Do you think technology improves the time you spend with your family? Why or why not?

Language development

Language development

INVERSION

Inversion is used to create emphasis, or to stress that something is unique or special. It occurs when an adverbial (e.g., *only, never, not*) is placed at the beginning of a sentence and the normal positions of the verb and subject are changed.

adverbial verb subject

Rarely has *such* ***a phenomenon*** *been seen.*

Compare with the normal word order: *Such* ***a phenomenon has rarely*** *been seen.*

Inversion is used:

- After certain phrases with *not*

  Not only *does a ritual convey a sense of "who we are" as a group,* ***(but) it also*** *makes the family feel like they belong together.*

- After certain phrases with *only*

  Only now *are the effects becoming apparent.*

  Only when *the rituals occupy an important part in each individual's mind, do they give the family its own meaning.*

- After certain phrases with *no*

  At no time *did we realize it was going to leave such a legacy.*

  No sooner *had it arrived on the market,* ***than*** *competitors were forced to change their approach to cell phone design.*

- After frequency adverbs *rarely, seldom, hardly, ever, never.*

  Never before *had a device revolutionized the market.*

1 Complete these sentences with a single word.

1 Not ______ was he a great leader, he also revolutionized the economy.

2 At ______ time during his days in the laboratory did he imagine he would make such a discovery.

3 ______ before had the world seen a groundbreaking idea such as this.

4 Only ______ is it considered to be of international importance.

5 No ______ had he finished this great project than he began the next one.

2 Rewrite these sentences starting with the words in parentheses.

1 There will never be a technological revolution again. (never again)

2 Apple revolutionized the phone industry and created the tablet industry. (not only)

3 Phone companies release the latest model and then bring a newer one out. (no sooner)

4 Computers weren't available to the general public until Microsoft® Windows was launched. (not until)

5 You rarely meet anyone nowadays who doesn't have a computer. (rarely)

6 You can only understand someone's technological legacy by reading their biography and using their product. (only by)

7 My family has only recently started to pass on family mealtime rituals. (only recently)

COLLOCATIONS: *WAY*

Way can collocate (= go together) with other words to form phrases which mean different things. It is always better to learn a word and its collocations together.

Here are some collocations that go before and after the word *way*:

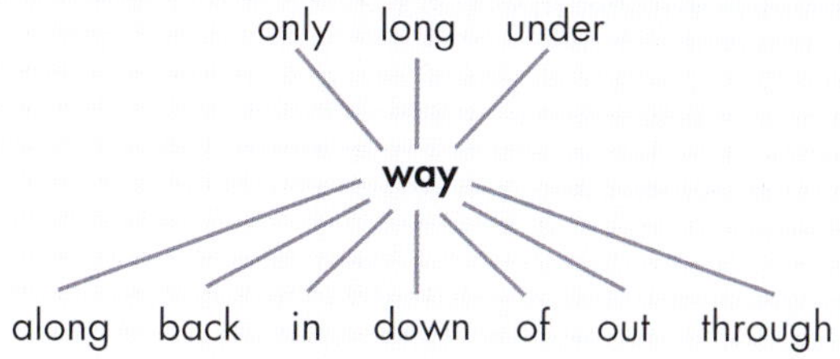

Look at the following examples of *way* from the listening texts:

And it's good for us in ***other ways****.* In this example, *way* refers to a method.

This was ***way back*** *in 1937.* Here, *way back* means a long time ago.

1 Read the following sentences and complete the collocations with one of the words in the box.

give	go	have	in	into	long	on	toward

1 A new iPhone model is ____________ **its way**.
2 mp3 downloads are outselling CDs by a ____________ **way**.
3 When you graduate, the **best way** ____________ a full-time job is doing an internship.
4 Douglas Englebart knew that using a mouse to interact with a computer was the **way to** ____________.
5 The music industry is ____________ **a bad way** due to downloading technology.
6 The mp4 player will eventually ____________ **way to** other technology.
7 You ____________ **a way with** giving presentations. Could you help me with mine?
8 The introduction of Windows **went a long way** ____________ making Microsoft the market leader.

2 Match the collocations from exercise 1 with their definitions below.

a be able to do something well ____________
b be replaced by something ____________
c going to be available soon ____________
d contribute a lot ____________
e a large amount ____________
f in an unhealthy condition ____________
g a situation that allows you to achieve something ____________
h the best method ____________

3 Which of these collocations are the most informal? Which ones could be used in more formal speaking or writing?

4 Work with a partner. Take turns testing each other on the collocations and their definitions.

SPEAKING Making a speech about a person who has left a legacy

You are going to practice highlighting important information using repetition of grammar and contrastive pairs. You will also learn how to pause for emphasis while speaking. Then you are going to use these skills to make a speech on behalf of your university about a person who has left a legacy.

Pronunciation skill

PAUSING FOR DRAMATIC EMPHASIS

Speakers often make a slight pause between groups of words. This pausing allows the content to be broken into "chunks" which are more easily processed by listeners. Pausing for emphasis also helps the speaker emphasize important information, and it works much like punctuation in written English.

1 **Look at the sentences below and predict where the pauses for emphasis will occur.**

1 A family mealtime ritual could be a symbolic act; it could involve objects, or it could be conversations.

2 Sure, it was the size of a room and today's tablets can fit in your pocket, but still, it's pretty impressive.

3 No sooner do phone companies release the latest model than a newer one comes out.

4 Only by reading someone's biography and using their product can you understand their technological legacy.

2 2.06 **Listen and check your answers. Practice saying the sentences aloud, pausing for emphasis. What is the main stressed word in each section?**

Speaking skill

EMPHASIZING IMPORTANT INFORMATION—REPETITION AND CONTRASTIVE PAIRS

Apart from pausing, there are other techniques to highlight and emphasize important information in speech. Here are two more devices.

Repetition of grammar

Speakers often repeat grammatical forms to emphasize a main point or conclusion. This repetition often occurs three times and is referred to as "tripling" or "the power of three."

A family mealtime ritual ***could*** *be a symbolic act, it* ***could*** *involve objects, or it* ***could*** *be conversations.*

Something from ***the past****, that is handed down to us from* ***the past****, or that happens in* ***the past.***

Contrastive pairs

Speakers choose to use contrastive pairs to show some real distinction between two points, or to show a clear link between two things that would not normally be connected.

It was the ***size of a room****, and today's tablets can* ***fit in your pocket****, but still, it's pretty impressive.*

1 2.07 **Listen to some clips from speeches. Decide whether they include repetition of grammar or contrastive pairs to add emphasis.**

2 **Choose two or three topics. Think of a key issue related to each topic and create a sentence that uses repetition or contrastive pairs for emphasis.**

SPEAKING TASK

BRAINSTORM

As part of a series of commemorative lectures, you are going to make a speech on behalf of your university faculty about a person who has left a legacy. Consider this question with a partner and make a list.

What qualities does a person need to have to leave a legacy?

PLAN

Working individually, think of a person you know who left a great legacy. This could be a famous person from your country, a friend, or a family member. Use a mind map to guide you. If the person is not well known to other people, you will really need to persuade listeners about the merits of the person through reason and evidence.

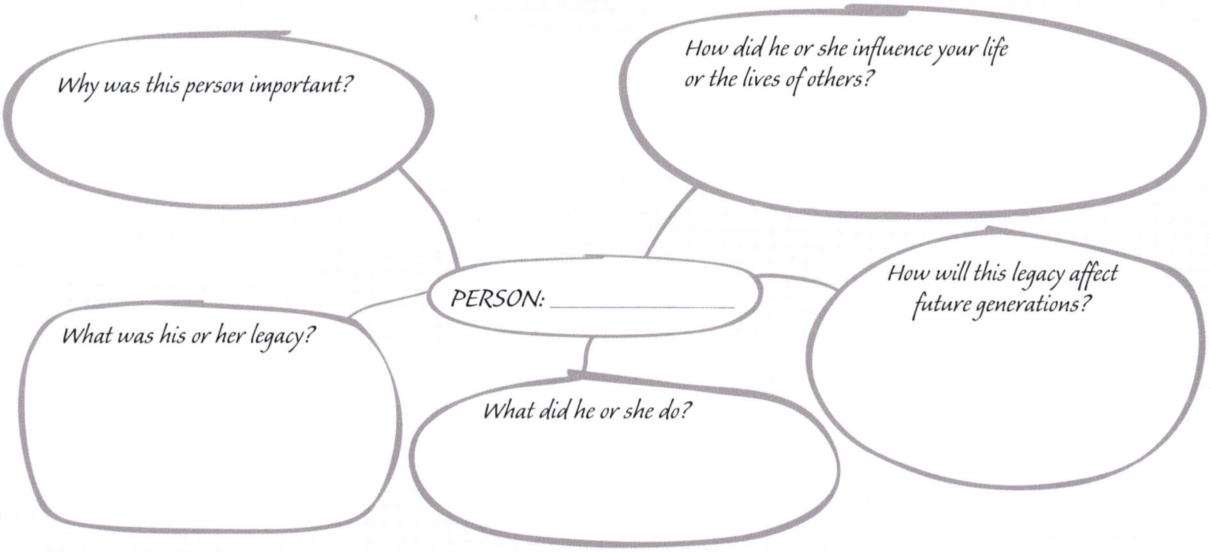

You are going to give a three-minute speech about this person. Choose the information you want to emphasize or highlight, and prepare some sentences using inversion and other ways of highlighting important information. Don't forget to maintain an overall structure for each point you cover—state your main idea, give examples and reasons, and then summarize your point.

SPEAK

Practice your speech with a partner. Give each other feedback on the speech. Consider:

- Is the structure of the presentation of each point clear? Point → Supporting examples and evidence → Conclusion
- Use of devices such as: inversion, stress, repetition, academic verbs, juncture, nominalization
- Is there any extra source material that could support the speech?

SHARE

Work in small groups. Deliver your speech to the group.

When you listen to your classmates' speeches, take some notes and ask them some questions about the source of their information.

The author's position

by Stella Cottrell

When we read, watch television or listen to people talking, we are presented with other people's arguments. Underlying those arguments are points of view or 'positions' that they aim to convey to us, their audience.

Note how the positions of the authors above relate to the overall arguments below.

Key terms: Argument

The word 'argument' is used in two ways in critical thinking:

- **Contributing arguments.** Individual reasons are referred to as 'arguments' or 'contributing arguments'.
- **The overall argument.** This is composed of contributing arguments, or reasons. The overall argument presents the author's position. The term 'line of reasoning' is used to refer to a set of reasons, or contributing arguments, structured to support the overall argument.

Overall argument	Contributing arguments
(1) Longer prison sentences should be introduced.	Heavy punishments deter criminals. Current penalties for crime are too lenient and don't deter criminals. Since prison sentences were reduced, crime has increased. Victims need to see that perpetrators of crimes are punished.

Overall argument	Contributing arguments
(2) Increasing prison sentences is not the way to stop crime.	Crime was high even when punishments were more weighty. Prison teaches people how to be more skilled as criminals. Criminals who are imprisoned are more likely to take part in increasingly serious crime when released. Most crime is committed by people who are illiterate and lack work-related skills. Education rather than punishment is needed.

Overall argument	Contributing arguments
(3) We should invest more in space travel.	Many discoveries have come about through space travel. It is important for us to learn more about the universe we live in. The fuel needed for space travel may not be around for much longer so we should use it while we have the chance.

Overall argument	Contributing arguments
(4) We should stop investing in space travel.	Space travel is expensive and the costs far outweigh the benefits. There are much more urgent projects that need investment more than space travel. Better alternatives for fuel for space travel may be available in the future.

Expanse

CRITICAL THINKING	Differentiating between fact and opinion Identifying statements that need justification
LANGUAGE DEVELOPMENT	Attitude adverbials Abstract nouns
PRONUNCIATION	Word stress: abstract nouns formed from adjectives
SPEAKING	Negotiating

Discussion point

Discuss these questions with a partner.

1 Why do you think many people are impressed with things that are on a grand scale? Do you believe that bigger is better? Is this belief universal across all cultures?

2 Think about the largest or longest examples of:

a building   a jewel   a mountain   a river   an airplane

Why do these things interest people? What can this tell us about our culture and ourselves?

3 Have attitudes to size changed in your country recently? Think about:

amounts of food people eat   cars   families   salaries

Vocabulary preview

1 **Complete the sentences with the words in the box.**

aloof colossal considerable extensive gargantuan
high up proximity remoteness transcontinental vast

1 The first ______________ railroad in the world was the Pacific Railroad, which connected Iowa in the Midwestern United States with the Pacific Ocean.
2 Mount Everest can be described as a mountain of ______________ proportions.
3 Technology is the key to overcoming the ______________ of places such as Alaska or Siberia.
4 He has an ______________ knowledge of Russian art history.
5 The hurricane caused ______________ damage to all coastal towns.
6 They really are friendly people. However, they are a little ______________ in the beginning, you know, distant.
7 The town's ______________ to the sea made fishing an important source of income.
8 These animals are ______________ in scale, ranging from five to seven meters in length.
9 Exploring the ______________ expanse of our galaxy is humankind's next adventure in space.
10 There is nothing more beautiful than looking down on a valley from ______________ on a mountaintop.

2 **Which three words are synonyms of *enormous*?**

LISTENING 1 The Trans-Siberian Railway

Before you listen

Discuss these questions with a partner.

1 What is the furthest you have ever traveled …
… by car? … by plane? … by train?
2 What is the best way to travel between cities within your country?
3 What transportation links does your city have—e.g., a railway station, an airport, a port, or access to a freeway? How have these links benefited the city?
What drawbacks have they brought?

ACADEMIC KEYWORDS		
extensive	(adj)	/ɪk'stensɪv/
largely	(adv)	/'lardʒli/
means	(n)	/minz/

Listening

2.08 **Listen to a podcast about why the Trans-Siberian Railway is considered to be so special. What do the following numbers refer to?**

1 9,289
2 seven
3 two
4 ten
5 72
6 80
7 1.5 million
8 12

Critical thinking skill

DIFFERENTIATING BETWEEN FACT AND OPINION

We need to establish whether information is based on fact or opinion.

A **fact** is supported by evidence or can be easily proven to be true through observation, experience, or comparison against evidence.

An **opinion** may be the point of view of an individual person.

Opinions are often signaled by: *From my point of view …, To my mind …, I would say …, As far as I am concerned …*

An opinion can also be held by a large group, signaled by: *It is popularly believed that …, People often claim that …, Many people believe that …*

However, sometimes there are no signal words or phrases, and sometimes opinions are also supported by "evidence," so you need to use other ways to ascertain that a statement is opinion and not fact.

- Consider any experience or knowledge you have of the topic. Ask yourself whether the statement fits with what you know to be true.
- Listen for any evidence presented by the speaker. Ask yourself whether the evidence is enough to prove the statement.

1 2.09 **Complete the first two rows of the chart with your own ideas. Then listen to two extracts from the podcast to complete the chart.**

	Statement 1: Russia is a huge country.	Statement 2: Russian people are friendly and interesting.
Do you have any experience or knowledge of the topic?		
Does the statement fit with your experience or knowledge?		
Is there any language to signal opinion?		
What evidence is presented (if any)?		
Does the evidence prove the statement? Why or why not?		
Is it fact or opinion?		

2 **Look at the following sentences. Use the information that you heard in the podcast to decide if they are based on fact (*F*) or opinion (*O*).**

1 The Trans-Siberian Railway played a vital part in uniting Russia as a nation. ___
2 Traveling on the Trans-Siberian is a positive experience. ___
3 The railway plays a crucial role in Russia's infrastructure. ___
4 The train is the only option for traveling long distances for most Russians. ___
5 The Trans-Siberian provides many people with a means to make a living. ___
6 The food from the restaurant is not good value for the money. ___

3 2.08 **Listen to the whole interview again and check your answers with a partner.**

Developing critical thinking

Discuss these questions in a group.

1 What are the advantages and disadvantages of large-scale transportation connections like the Trans-Siberian Railway? How can they help a country?
2 Does traveling across a large country help you to understand its people and culture? How can it change the traveler? Give reasons and examples.
3 Does a large country with a small population have advantages over a small country with a large population?

LISTENING 2 Why do people climb mountains?

Before you listen

1 **Work with a partner. Look at the following adjectives and decide which you would use to describe climbing a mountain.**

artistic	challenging	compelling	cooperative	creative	deadly
exhausting	hazardous	painful	picturesque	rewarding	satisfying

2 **Explain the reasons for your choice of adjectives.**

3 **Which adjectives did you NOT choose? Explain why.**

ACADEMIC KEYWORDS

symbolize	(v)	/'sɪmbəˌlaɪz/
extend	(v)	/ɪk'stend/
interaction	(v)	/ˌɪntər'ækʃən/

Listening

2.10 **Listen to a talk from a university mountaineering club on why people climb mountains. Which of the adjectives you chose in *Before you listen* correspond to what the speaker says?**

Critical thinking skill

IDENTIFYING STATEMENTS THAT NEED JUSTIFICATION

Some statements (or claims) stand alone and do not require further justification. We can call these **self-evident.**

Mountain climbing is problematic, hazardous, and often painful.

The speaker does not elaborate further because there is no need to do so. He assumes that his listeners know enough about mountain climbing to understand why it is problematic, hazardous, and often painful. Sometimes a self-evident statement is proceeded by a signal such as: *Naturally, …, Obviously, …,* or *Of course, …*

However some statements require justification; otherwise they may leave the listener puzzled.

Statement: *Climbing allows us to create our own reward sequence.* The listener might wonder what "reward sequence" could mean here.

Justification: *An uphill slope represents an incentive and a peak symbolizes achievement.*

When taking notes in a lecture, a common mistake is to write down a striking statement that the lecturer made, but not make a note of the justification. Then on reviewing the notes later, it is not clear what the lecturer meant.

It is important to distinguish between self-evident statements and those that need justification. If it is not self-evident, you need to note the justification as well as the statement.

1 **Check the statements that require justification.**

1 ☐ People climb mountains because they love being part of a team.
2 ☐ The challenge of climbing represents the challenges in life.
3 ☐ Climbing pushes us to our physical limits.
4 ☐ Climbing allows a person to get to know him or herself better.
5 ☐ Climbing allows us to appreciate the beauty of nature.
6 ☐ Climbing is artistic.

2 2.10 **Listen to the talk again. Look at the statements you checked. What justifications does the speaker give for them?**

3 **Compare your answers with a partner.**

Developing critical thinking

1 **Discuss these questions in a group.**

1 What do you think is the single biggest motivating factor for people who climb mountains? Is it one of the reasons mentioned by the speaker? Can you think of other activities that people do for a similar reason?

2 Did the speaker encourage you to consider climbing a mountain? Why or why not?

2 **Think about the ideas from *Listening 1* and *Listening 2*, and discuss these questions in a group.**

1 Look at the things in the box and decide if you would prefer them to be large or small. Compare your answers and give reasons for your choices.

your bedroom	your car	your city/town
your group of friends	your house	your television

2 Throughout history, people have achieved many huge physical feats, such as landing on the moon, reaching the South Pole, and climbing Mount Everest. Make a list of other physical achievements. What benefits have they brought to humanity?

Language development

ATTITUDE ADVERBIALS

A number of adverbs or adverbial phrases can be used to describe the speaker's attitude to what follows or what goes before in a sentence. Most of them can be placed at the beginning of a clause, or within it.

***Naturally**, climbing also compels us to explore and extend our physical limitations.*

*It is **naturally** exciting to reach the summit, but this is only an end.*

Some adverbs can be used before ***enough***:

oddly, funnily, strangely, surprisingly

***Oddly enough**, there is also another side to climbing a mountain that many people would not think of, and that is creativity.*

Some abstract nouns of emotion (cf. p. 73) can be used after ***much to my*** …

surprise, delight, disgust, dismay, horror

***Much to my delight**, I have witnessed the most breathtaking landscapes.*

1 Complete these sentences by placing an attitude adverbial in an appropriate position.

honestly ideally not surprisingly personally understandably undoubtedly

1. Most of the quality road systems are based around Moscow and Saint Petersburg.
2. The remoteness of this vast land area isolated many groups of Russians across two continents, making it very difficult to rule as a nation.
3. I believe the Russians are friendly people.
4. Climbing is a dangerous pursuit.
5. You should go climbing with a team.
6. I have never seen anything as beautiful as a sunrise from the top of a mountain crest.

2 Continue each of the stories by writing a second sentence with an appropriate attitude adverbial.

1. I woke up and looked out of the train window.
   Much to my surprise, …
2. I looked down to make sure my climbing partner was OK.
3. I was the first to arrive for our first lecture of the year. I sat down and waited.
4. The boat hit a huge rock and sank within five minutes.

3 Compare your sentences with a partner. How similar are they? What are the differences?

Language development

ABSTRACT NOUNS

An abstract noun is a name given to an emotion, ideal, or idea. It has no physical presence. You cannot see, smell, hear, taste, or touch it.

*The **remoteness** of this vast land area isolated many groups of Russians across two continents.*

Many abstract nouns are the root for other words.

surprise (n) → *surprise* (v), *surprising* (adj)   *horror* (n) → *horrify* (v), *horrifying* (adj)

Other abstract nouns are formed from a root adjective by adding a suffix.

remote (adj) → *remote**ness*** (n)   *original* (adj) → *original**ity*** (n)

1 Use the correct form of the words in parentheses to complete these extracts from the recordings. Two of the abstract nouns require a negative prefix.

1 Considering the history of the Trans-Siberian and what the *possibility* of its ______________ meant to the Russian ruling family at the end of the nineteenth century, I would say that it has had a remarkable role to play in the ______________ of Russia as a nation. (possible, exist, develop)

2 They can really shame you with their ______________. (kind)

3 I certainly feel that the special railway refers to the ______________ it has for the people. (important)

4 What happened was that the economic ______________ in the years following the collapse of the Soviet regime brought a lot of ______________ and ______________ to the whole country. (active, employ, hard)

5 Cooperation is needed to succeed, and ______________ must prevail. (unite)

6 Climbing allows us to create our own reward sequence, a source of ______________ we can go back to again and again. (satisfy)

7 An uphill slope represents an incentive and a peak symbolizes ______________. (achieve)

2 Place the original root words from exercise 1 in the correct column below.

-ment	-action	-y	-ness	-ence	-ance	-ship	-ity
							possible

3 Complete the sentences with an abstract noun from exercise 1.

1 What started my homesickness was the ______________ before the course started. I was really bored.

2 The Trans-Siberian has partially solved the problem of ______________ in Siberia.

3 Being in the open air gives me a tremendous sense of ______________.

4 The university climbing club came into ______________ in 1989.

5 Finishing a climb always gives me a feeling of ______________.

6 The aim of these activities is to help students with the ______________ of new skills.

Speaking skills

SPEAKING Organizing a cultural program

You are going to practice identifying word stress to produce good rhythm when speaking. You will also learn how to negotiate compromise to reduce conflict. Then you are going to use these skills to organize a cultural program for overseas students at your university.

Pronunciation skill

WORD STRESS: ABSTRACT NOUNS FORMED FROM ADJECTIVES

When you learn a new word, it is important to learn its stress pattern, as an incorrectly stressed word might impede understanding.

With abstract nouns formed from adjectives (cf. p. 73), there is a clear stress pattern to follow, so you can usually work out the correct stress if you are familiar with the root adjective.

1 **Underline the stressed syllable in the following words.**

1	possible	possibility	5	develop	development
2	satisfy	satisfaction	6	important	importance
3	exist	existence	7	inactive	inactivity
4	achieve	achievement	8	employ	employment

2 2.11 **Listen and check your answers. Which endings cause a change in stress? Where does the new stressed syllable go?**

Speaking skill

NEGOTIATING

When working as part of a group, a certain amount of negotiation will be required when discussing ideas or making suggestions.

Making suggestions

Use modal verbs such as *could*, *should*, *would*, and *might*, and phrases such as *perhaps*, *I think*, and *maybe* to make polite suggestions.

I would like to suggest that we … *I think perhaps we could …*

Part of the negotiation process is asking for the other person's opinion and checking whether they agree or not.

Checking

Are you happy with that? *What do you think about that?*

Asking why

Why have you suggested that?

What's the reason for ___ing …?

Asking why not

What would be wrong with doing this?

Why would you object to …?

1 2.12 **Listen to a conversation. Check the expressions you hear in the *Negotiating* box and say what the speakers decided to do in the end.**

2 **Choose two of the following situations. Work with a partner and negotiate what to do.**

- You are going to meet for lunch.
- You want to meet up to do some sports.
- You need to arrange a school reunion celebration.

SPEAKING TASK

BRAINSTORM

Work in groups of four. You need to organize a five-day educational cultural program for 20 overseas students who are going to enter your university next semester. They are required to visit sites of historical, political, and cultural importance.

Make a list under the following headings:

- The best places to visit that have historical/political/cultural importance. (Remember the students are not tourists on a sightseeing tour, so the sites don't need to be conventional tourist attractions.)
- Reasons for visiting each place — what is its significance?

PLAN

Work with a partner from your group. Plan a cultural program for the foreign students. You need to take into account the following:

- You must organize a program for four days.
- You must organize a minimum of two visits per day.
- You must include a short description of each visit site and highlight its importance.
- You have an unlimited budget.
- You must prioritize one area of the program that might need a risk assessment.

SPEAK

You hear the news that your budget has been cut to zero. Also, students now only need to participate in one activity per day. Work with a new partner from a different group. You must negotiate a compromise between your programs to finalize a cultural program together. Make suggestions, check, and ask follow-up *why* questions.

SHARE

Work with your original partners from the brainstorm stage. Explain your cultural program and justify any statements you made to explain why you made the decisions you did.

STUDY SKILLS Organizing your personal study online

Getting started

Discuss these questions with a partner.

1 How do you organize your personal study? Think of times, places, or the amount of time you spend on different subjects.

2 Do you prefer to study alone or with other people? Why?

3 Do you find it easy or difficult to search for and find suitable information on the Internet?

Scenario

Read about Haru, a first-year university student who has received negative feedback on his first assignments. What advice would you give him?

Haru has received some negative feedback on his first two university assignments. He has been told that he must do more in-depth research on his own to support his points. His tutor made it very clear that only doing the core course reading is not enough to attain the level required to pass the module.

Before starting university, he always relied on his teachers to provide him with resources and managed to obtain good grades by doing the homework they gave him. He had felt a little insecure about the prospect of working more independently. However, he now knows that he must become more responsible for his own learning and that there is a vast range of online resources that he can access.

As part of the assignment feedback, Haru has been given links to academic search engines. Although these links are a useful first step, he is unsure how to do an effective search for the articles and sources he needs. He also has a very busy schedule during the week, so he has doubts about how much time he will have to do his independent research. Furthermore, he tends to use his computer for gaming and social networking and these are huge distractions while he is online. Another of Haru's concerns is finding a suitable place to work; the library is normally full on weekdays, and he finds it difficult to concentrate at home.

Consider it

Which of these tips about organizing your personal study online have you tried?

1 **Formulate an effective search strategy**. Define what you want the articles to be about by selecting relevant keywords. Organize how you want the keywords to be entered. Use the words ***and*** and ***or*** with **parentheses** to link your keywords. For example, *Trans-Siberian Railway* ***and*** (*Russian infrastructure* **or** *Novosibirsk*).

2 **Set out a study routine.** Plan your study week to include seven days. Make time for study, but allow time for socializing, relaxing, and other commitments. Plan your study periods according to the time that is best for you. Some people prefer mornings; others work better in the evenings.

3 **Set realistic study goals.** Use a calendar and set real deadlines, and keep to them—you could use an online organizer to keep everything together on your computer. Know when your assignment is due and plan the amount of work you need to do and the days you can do it. Do your assignment step-by-step according to your deadlines. Do not procrastinate!

4 **Minimize distractions.** Find a private space at home where you can close the door and work in peace. Consider what times or days the library is quieter so that you can work there undisturbed. Remember to respect your study time, so do not open web pages not related to your study.

5 **Foster motivation.** Remember that this is your own research time and motivation must come from you, so try to find ways to encourage yourself. Think about the satisfaction of producing a complete assignment, find a study partner or study group you can share your research with, and think about giving yourself a reward on completion of your work. Anything that can motivate you through the process will help you stay focused.

6 **Use your new knowledge.** Connect what you have learned through research to what you already know. Add this information to your lecture notes on the topic. Explain your new knowledge to someone else in order to develop a better understanding. You could record a podcast for your study group explaining what you have learned.

Over to you

Discuss these questions with a partner.

1 Which of the tips in *Consider it* do you think are most useful for you? Give reasons.

2 How do you motivate yourself to study? Give examples.

3 Do you have other suggestions on how to organize your personal study?

Change

CRITICAL THINKING	Maximizing language Recognizing implicit assumptions
LANGUAGE DEVELOPMENT	Expressing change Gradable adjectives
PRONUNCIATION	Intonation and tonic prominence
SPEAKING	Adding points to an argument

Discussion point

Discuss these questions with a partner.

1 When was the last time you experienced a major change in your life?

2 Do you react positively or negatively to change?

3 Why do some people find change difficult and others enjoy it? How is it possible to adapt positively to change?

Vocabulary preview

1 Circle the correct option to best define the word in bold.

1 If the level of water in a river **fluctuates**, it changes *frequently / dramatically / rarely.*

2 When a baby bird, fish, or insect **hatches**, it *dies / comes out of an egg / becomes mature.*

3 A **subterranean** life form lives *in water / in trees / under the ground.*

4 When a creature **reproduces**, it *has offspring / changes color / changes form.*

5 An insect's **exoskeleton** is a hard covering *inside its body / outside its body / on its head.*

6 An animal's **lifespan** is the average amount of time *it is expected to live / it takes to reproduce / it takes to become an adult.*

7 If you are involved in a **transaction**, you are *changing from one thing into another / buying or selling something / communicating with someone.*

8 A **conundrum** is a *problem with no apparent solution / catastrophic change / surprising development.*

2 Which word in bold in exercise 1 is related to change?

LISTENING 1 Metamorphosis—the secrets behind nature's amazing change

metamorphosis
/ˌmetəˈmɔrfəsɪs/
NOUN
a major change in the physical form of an insect or other animal as it develops

Before you listen

Read the definition of metamorphosis. How much do you know about the process? Fill in the table below.

What I know	
What I would like to know	
How I can find out	

Listening

2.13 Listen to a lecture about the metamorphosis of the cicada. Complete the notes on the next page with the numbers in the box.

5	20	13 or 17	100	68	1.5	4

ACADEMIC KEYWORDS

considerable	(adj)	/kənˈsɪd(ə)rəb(ə)l/
emerge	(v)	/ɪˈmɜː(r)dʒ/
model	(n)	/ˈmɑd(ə)l/

- *Annual cicada appears every year, while periodical appears every (1) ___________ years.*
- *Cicada nymphs go through (2) ___________ stages of molting underground. Then they climb the nearest tree.*
- *Lifespan above ground is (3) ___________ weeks long, and has one purpose: reproduction.*
- *Males sing a song to attract females in "chorus trees." Singing can reach (4) ___________ decibels and can be heard from up to (5) ___________ km. away.*
- *When mating is over, females lay (6) ___________ eggs in the branches of young trees. Eggs hatch and nymphs drop to ground. Cycle begins again.*
- *Long life cycles helped avoid the colder summers (cicadas need temperatures of (7) ___________ degrees to live). But this doesn't explain the 13- and 17-year cycles.*

Critical thinking skill

MAXIMIZING LANGUAGE

To make a point more forcefully, speakers might use exaggerated language. This is also called *maximizing language*. This can mean:

- using more extreme adjectives: *huge* instead of *big*
- emphasizing adjectives with adverbs: *utterly breathtaking …*
- repeating a word: *a **very very very** important day*
- using superlatives: ***the most incredible** thing*
- using metaphorical language: *Changes occur here **in the blink of an eye**.*

When a speaker uses maximizing language, it is often an indication of the importance of what he or she is saying, and can signal key points in a lecture or presentation.

1 2.14 **Read the text below. Then listen to the first part of the lecture again and write down the differences between the text and what the speaker actually says.**

After waiting underground for 17 years, these insects come from the ground and go to the nearest tree. They climb the tree to release more of their kind into a few acres of land.

We will look at the life cycle of the periodical cicada today in order to consider a question that has puzzled experts. Why do they wait so long to complete their metamorphosis? And why do they all emerge at the same time? Let's start by looking at the 17-year-old variety's lifestyle.

2 **Look at the differences you noted in exercise 1. Where does the speaker use maximizing language? What words or phrases does he use? Why does the lecturer use exaggerated language?**

Developing critical thinking

Discuss these questions in a group.

1 What aspect of the periodical cicada's life cycle do you find the most surprising or fascinating?

2 What other fascinating natural changes or processes do you know about? Why are they so interesting?

3 What is the most interesting / most frightening / strangest natural phenomenon you have ever seen?

LISTENING 2 A global tax on changing money?

Before you listen

1 Discuss these questions with a partner.

1 How many currencies can you name in one minute? Make a list.
2 Do you know how much your national currency is worth compared to other currencies (for example, the rate of exchange with the U.S. dollar or the British pound)?
3 How do changes in currency affect you?

2 Complete the information about the money market. Have you heard of this before? Do you think it is a good way for banks to use money?

lending profit risky speculation

The *money market* refers to business activities in which banks and other financial institutions make money by (1) _____________ money to other organizations. Historically, the money market has been a place where much (2) _____________ occurs: this involves (3) _____________ financial transactions in an attempt to (4) _____________ from short-term fluctuations in the value of different currencies.

Listening

2.15 You are going to listen to a radio debate about a tax on exchanging currencies. Listen and choose the correct answer.

1 The original plan for a currency tax was
  a to increase the cost of trading in currencies.
  b to discourage speculation.
  c both a and b.
2 Which of the following claims is made?
  a Eighty percent of all world trade is currency trade.
  b Some 1.5 trillion dollars are exchanged daily in money markets.
  c Financiers are solely responsible for the recent economic crises.
3 A small tax on money exchanges
  a could raise up to 300 billion dollars.
  b could raise around ten million dollars.
  c could reduce world poverty by 0.1%.
4 According to the speaker, the problem with an international law about currency tax is
  a rich countries would create the law.
  b it would be hard to enforce.
  c the United Nations would not accept it.
5 Which of the following do the speakers actually agree on?
  a Currency speculation is inevitable in the world's economy.
  b They want to see a better world.
  c Their arguments are both idealistic. (= believing very firmly in something which is good, but probably impossible to achieve)

ACADEMIC KEYWORDS

argument	(n)	/'ɑrgjəmənt/
frequently	(adv)	/'frikwəntli/
rely	(v)	/rɪ'laɪ/

Critical thinking skill

RECOGNIZING IMPLICIT ASSUMPTIONS

In critical thinking, implicit assumptions are facts or beliefs that are taken for granted in the presentation of an argument. They underlie (= are the reason for something) the argument, but are not stated explicitly.

If the government increases tax on these products, the resulting decline in sales will hit the industry hard at this time.

The implicit assumption that underlies the above example is that increasing tax on a product will lead to a decrease in sales of the product. This is a reasonable assumption (if a product is more expensive, people are less likely to buy it), but it is not necessarily true in this case (it's possible that sales of the product will not be affected by the higher cost).

If you can recognize when an implicit assumption has been made, you can decide for yourself whether you agree with it rather than simply accepting the speaker's argument.

1 2.15 **Listen to the debate again and complete the three extracts from the dialogue.**

1 If suddenly your currency is in demand, and value ________________, then the cost of your goods to other countries goes up, too. That can have a ________________ on consumer goods, agriculture and ultimately, on the money in ________________.

2 If we ________________ tax on trading, either for money trading or any other kind of trading, it will ________________ an economy. This will ________________ especially the weaker economies.

3 What Mrs. Mawer suggests sounds very noble, but the truth is that countries that receive ________________of financial aid become accustomed to ________________ that income. What we need is for those countries to ________________ their own efficient economy.

2 **Circle the correct option to best describe the implicit assumption made by the speaker in each extract in exercise 1.**

1 Changes in the cost of consumer goods are **positive** / **negative** / **inevitable**.

2 Tax **discourages** / **encourages** / **has no effect** *on* trading.

3 It is a **bad thing** / **a good thing** / **efficient** for poorer countries to rely on financial aid.

Developing critical thinking

1 **Discuss these questions in a group.**

1 Does the value of your country's currency change frequently? What problems might a fluctuating currency cause?

2 How do you think banks, financial institutions, and governments should address problems like tax evasion and reducing poverty?

2 **Think about the ideas from *Listening 1* and *Listening 2*, and discuss these questions in a group.**

1 Some people say that in the twenty-first century the world is undergoing a significant metamorphosis. Do you agree? List some of the changes that support this argument in these areas: politics, society, technology, finance, environment, and climate.

2 Compared to other countries in the world, do you think your country has changed rapidly or slowly in the last 50 years? What changes have been made, and how do you feel about these changes?

3 Are you positive or negative about change in general?

Language development

EXPRESSING CHANGE

Change is a concept that is discussed in many academic contexts. There are a number of ways that it is expressed—formally, informally, and with reference to specific subjects or processes. The following verbs are commonly used in expressing change:

- *adapt*—to change something to fit with a specific situation
- *adjust*—to change something slightly
- *convert*—to change something so it can be used for a different purpose
- *transform*—to change something completely so that it looks or works much better
- *vary*—to be different in different situations.

Note that most of these verbs have several slightly different meanings. Refer to a dictionary for full definitions.

1 Replace the verb *change* with a synonym. More than one answer may be possible.

1 These recipes can be easily **changed** so that they are suitable for vegetarians.
2 The engineers were working as quickly as possible to **change** all the programs in time for the new update that will roll out in April.
3 The fees for services like these can **change** from country to country.
4 The new authors in Brazil are looking to **change** the nature of South American contemporary fiction.
5 You can **change** the brightness and contrast on your screen by using the up and down arrows.
6 This summer they **changed** the spare bedroom into an office.

2 Work with a partner. Try to think of three other verbs meaning "to change," using a thesaurus if necessary. Find their exact definition in a dictionary. Do they usually refer to large or small changes? Which of the meanings listed in the *Expressing change* box do they match most closely?

3 Work with a partner. Choose three of the questions to ask and answer below.

1 What kinds of historical event can completely transform a country? Can you think of examples?
2 Does your daily routine vary depending on the time of year?
3 If you lived in a completely different culture, would you find it easy to adapt your way of life?
4 How could you adjust your eating habits to make them a little healthier?
5 What changes could you make to convert an ordinary house into an eco-friendly one?

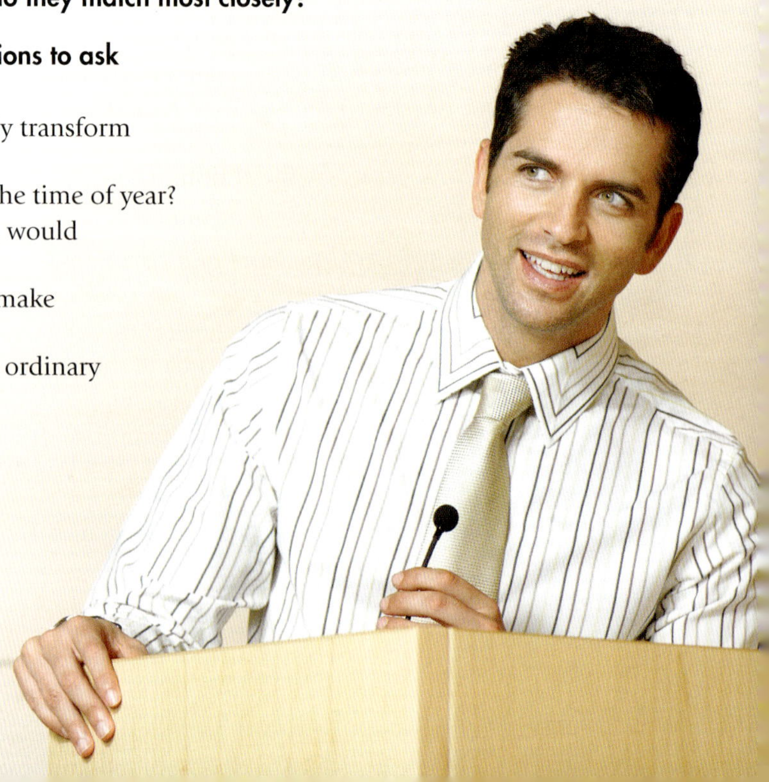

GRADABLE ADJECTIVES

Adjectives in English can be gradable or non-gradable.

Gradable adjectives can vary in intensity or grade. We use modifying adverbs to show this.

cold → a little cold, very cold, extremely cold

Non-gradable adjectives can be **absolute** (e.g., *alive*—you are either alive or not) or **extreme** (e.g., *colossal*).

Non-gradable adjectives cannot be used with adverbs such as *very, a little,* or *extremely*. They often stand alone.

~~a little~~ freezing

Non-gradable extreme adjectives can be used with non-grading adverbs, such as *absolutely, utterly,* or *completely*. This gives the non-gradable adjective more impact.

*It's **absolutely** freezing outside.*

Many non-gradable adjectives can also be used with adjectives meaning *almost,* such as *practically, virtually,* or *nearly.*

A typical mistake is to put the adverb *very* in front of non-gradable adjectives.

You are suggesting something that is ~~very~~ impossible.

1 **Cross out the word that cannot modify the adjective in bold.**

1	absolutely	virtually	very	practically	**impossible**
2	nearly	a little	completely	absolutely	**boiling**
3	practically	incredibly	extremely	very	**fast**
4	almost	a little	virtually	nearly	**dead**
5	very	a little	quite	utterly	**strong**

2 **Read the following extracts from a debate on technological change in education. Find the mistake in each extract.**

1 Not only is technology a forum for sharing and presenting existing knowledge, it also provides a very unique opportunity to create new knowledge. This creates superior knowledge.

2 There is an absolutely infinite choice of learning tools using technology, it's true. But it's also true that a quite huge choice of possible distractions exist. Social media, instant messaging, and online games can detract from learning.

3 Face-to-face learning is virtually important for many reasons, such as group work and real-world application of tasks. It's almost impossible to reproduce these conditions online.

4 Businesses and commercial interests are mainly responsible for many technological changes in the classroom. Teachers and students play a very miniscule part in these changes.

Speaking skills

SPEAKING Holding a debate about educational changes

You are going to practice intonation and sentence stress when giving replies to information. You will review how to add points to develop an argument. Then you are going to use these skills to hold a debate about changes in education systems.

Pronunciation skill

INTONATION AND TONIC PROMINENCE

In many English sentences, one syllable is often stressed more than the others. This means it is spoken more emphatically, through use of volume (more loudly), speed (more slowly), or tone (a higher tone). This is called the tonic prominence.

I want that one. (*that* is stressed.)

Syllables that come after the tonic prominence are often unstressed. These are called the tail of the tone unit.

I want that one on the left. (*one on the left* comes after the tonic prominence, and is unstressed.)

Long tails are often spoken quickly because they contain information that the speaker doesn't consider to be as important as the tonic prominence.

2.16 **Listen to the following exchanges and underline the tonic prominence in B's responses.**

1 **A:** I didn't understand what the professor was talking about.
  B: I had no idea what the professor was talking about.
2 **A:** Can you lend me your notes on the first lecture?
  B: I didn't take any notes on the first lecture.
3 **A:** We don't know if this tax will work.
  B: I don't think anybody knows if this tax will work.
4 **A:** You could set up laws to decide where the money goes.
  B: Yes, but who would enforce those laws to decide where the money goes?

Speaking skill

ADDING POINTS TO AN ARGUMENT

When presenting an argument in formal English, you can indicate that you are adding points or information to support your argument by using signaling words and phrases before the additional information, such as:
moreover, furthermore, besides, likewise, in addition, what is more …

Underline the signaling words or phrases in these sentences. Then number the sentences in order. Read aloud the paragraph using appropriate intonation.

a Moreover, the university does not have a lot of money to spare in these difficult economic times. ___
b I would like to argue that the proposed investment for a new student sports center is a terrible idea. ___
c The existing center is more than sufficient for student needs. ___
d My main reason is that we already have one. Why do we need another one? ___
e What is more, it's only five years old. ___

SPEAKING TASK

BRAINSTORM

"The new generation is digital, but our education is analog and needs to change."

What assumptions are behind each part of this quotation? Work with a partner and add to the lists in the table below.

New generation is digital	Education is analog and needs to change
Young people all have computers.	*Classrooms don't have computers.*

PLAN

You are going to hold a debate in response to the above quotation.

Form three groups.

Group 1: You agree with the statement.

Group 2: You disagree with the statement.

Group 3: You are the moderators of the debate. This requires you to provide opportunities for balanced discussion, stop any irrelevant or overly long turns, and encourage quieter members to speak out during the discussion.

Group 3 needs to set a time allowance in advance for each group to present their arguments.

Groups 1 and 2 prepare arguments and divide them between the speakers in the group. Think about:

- signaling the introduction of your ideas
- maximizing language to emphasize your points.

Group 3 prepares a checklist to evaluate the arguments. Use the checklist below, and add three more items to check.

		Comments or examples
Is this argument well structured?	Y/N	
Did the speakers provide supporting examples, reasons, and evidence?	Y/N	
Did the speakers summarize each point clearly?	Y/N	
	Y/N	
	Y/N	
	Y/N	

SPEAK

Hold the class debate.

Group 3: Introduce the debate.

Groups 1 and 2: Take turns presenting arguments for and against the statement. As you listen, write down the other group's main arguments.

After each group has presented their arguments, look at your notes. How could you argue against the other group's main argument? Present your counter-argument.

SHARE

At the end of the debate, group 3 decides which group made the best argument. Give feedback on the arguments presented by groups 1 and 2. Which arguments were the most convincing? Why?

Argument and disagreement

by Stella Cottrell

Argument is not the same as disagreement. You can disagree with someone else's position without pointing out why you disagree or persuading them to think differently. In critical thinking, there is a distinction between a position, an agreement, a disagreement and an argument.

Key terms

- **Position** A point of view.
- **Agreement** To concur with someone else's point of view.
- **Disagreement** To hold a different point of view from someone else.
- **Argument** Using reasons to support a point of view, so that known or unknown audiences may be persuaded to agree. An argument may include disagreement, but is more than simply disagreement if it is based on reasons.

Example

- *Position*: Genetically modified food really worries me. I don't think it should be allowed. [No reasons are given so this is simply a position.]
- *Agreement 1*: I don't know much about genetically modified food, but I agree with you.

Or

- *Agreement 2*: I know a lot about this subject and I agree with you. [No reasons are given so these are simply agreements.]
- *Disagreement*: That doesn't convince me. I think genetically modified food is really exciting. [No reasons are given so this is simply a disagreement.]
- *Argument 1*: Genetic engineering should be curtailed because there hasn't been sufficient research into what happens when new plant species are created.

Or

- *Argument 2*: The possibilities for improving crop yield through genetically modified food offer particular hope to those affected by food shortages. We should be pushing ahead to advance GMO technology.

The arguments above use reasons for the position held, to persuade others to the point of view. Note that these are simple arguments: they don't have extended lines of reasoning and they don't present any evidence to support their case. Without these, the power of the argument would have to depend on other factors such as tone of voice, body language or insider knowledge about the listener, such as that they had a vested interest in the outcome.

Flow

CRITICAL THINKING	Identifying counter-arguments Visual aids and diagrams
LANGUAGE DEVELOPMENT	Irregular plurals Words in context—working with concordance data
PRONUNCIATION	Intonation to express hesitation and doubt
SPEAKING	Softening criticism

Discussion point

Discuss these questions with a partner.

1 What river or other body of water is nearest to where you live? How would you describe it?

2 "In terms of global conflicts, water is the next oil." What do you understand by this statement? Do you agree?

3 Imagine you were without a water supply for six months. How would you manage?

Vocabulary preview

Read the sentences below and fill in the spaces with the words in the box.

aquatic	compelling	contamination	contemplating	displacement
economic stimulus	evaporation	intrinsic motivation	sobering	subjective

1 Many ________________ wildlife species are at risk from ambitious construction projects near rivers and the ocean.
2 ________________ and transpiration both involve the change from a liquid to a gaseous state.
3 Local residents are ________________ a protest against the proposed development.
4 A consequence of the warming of the North Pole is the ________________ of polar bears further south.
5 The vast scale of destruction of jungle habitats is a ________________ thought.
6 Soil ________________ has a lasting legacy on both flora and fauna.
7 The panda preservation activists made a ________________ case to stop logging.
8 ________________ is an important factor in being able to reach a goal.
9 I thought the professor's opinion was rather ________________, lacking concrete facts.
10 Governments cite the need for ________________, but not enough momentum gathers behind their proposals to make a difference.

LISTENING 1 Not worth a dam

Before you listen

1 **Look at these words and phrases. How might they be connected to dams?**

environmental costs	hydroelectric power	irrigation
renewable energy	river ecosystems	significant controversy

2 **Read the text and complete it with the words and phrases in exercise 1.**

A dam is a wall built across a river to stop the water from flowing. Dams have existed for thousands of years and have served various purposes, such as (1) ________________ and flood control. Dams also supply large amounts of (2) ________________, which accounts for almost 20% of the world's electricity, and more than 50% of the planet's (3) ________________. However, in recent times, dams have become the subject of (4) ________________ among environmentalists and local groups. The controversy arises mainly because of the local (5) ________________ of dams to (6) ________________ and local populations. Largely for this reason, new dam construction has declined, and dams have become less popular as a renewable energy source.

Listening

2.17 **Listen to someone talking about the construction of a big dam and answer these questions.**

1 Who is the woman speaking to?
2 What is the purpose of her talk?
3 What reasons does she give in support of her main argument?
4 What expression does she use to finish her talk?

ACADEMIC KEYWORDS

alternative	(adj)	/ɔl'tɜrnətɪv/
initial	(adj)	/ɪ'nɪʃ(ə)l/
permit	(v)	/pər'mɪt/

Critical thinking skill

IDENTIFYING COUNTER-ARGUMENTS

A strong academic argument will usually consider and evaluate points of view that oppose the argument, and present counter-arguments. By showing that he or she has considered and can refute or disprove alternative perspectives, a speaker strengthens his or her own argument.

A speaker will often use words and phrases such as these to signal that they are presenting an alternative view: *on the other hand, however, nonetheless, I would argue that, I would like to point out that.*

1 2.17 **Listen again. Check five arguments that the speaker mentions in favor of dams.**

1 ☐ The construction of the dam will stimulate the economy.
2 ☐ The dam will provide electricity for new businesses in the area.
3 ☐ The dam will bring more money and jobs to the area.
4 ☐ The environmental impact will be minimal.
5 ☐ Dams are an efficient water storage method.
6 ☐ The dam will prevent annual flooding.
7 ☐ Dams generate a lot of electricity.

2 **Match the speaker's arguments against dams below with the arguments in favor of dams in exercise 1.**

a Storing water underground is safer and more efficient. ____
b The investment in the project will cost more money than the government can afford. ____
c The damage to the local population outweighs the benefits. ____
d Alternative energy sources would have less impact on the local area. ____
e Damage to animals is significant and irreversible. ____

3 **Work with a partner. Read the arguments in favor of dams below. Then discuss how the speaker makes a counter-argument.**

1 Hydropower is far cheaper than other renewable energy sources, and hydroelectric dams can last up to a hundred years. They provide an excellent return on investment.
2 Dams protect wildlife from the dangers of flooding, and the reservoir created by a dam can be a fish habitat. Most animals that live near rivers are adaptable to natural flooding anyway.
3 Dams help fight global water shortages. Global warming has distorted rainfall. In some areas there are now great water shortages. Dam reservoirs provide an excellent solution to this by storing water.

Developing critical thinking

Discuss these questions in a group.

1 Which of the viewpoints presented above do you agree with? Why? Can you think of any more arguments that could be made in favor of dams? Can you think of a counter-argument for each one?
2 Can you think of other big construction projects, like dams, that are also the subject of controversy (for example, railway lines)? What are some of the arguments against them?
3 Do you ever speak up about controversial construction projects, or do you feel that they are part of an inevitable process of change that is out of your control?

LISTENING 2 The concept of flow

Before you listen

Look at the question below. How would you answer it? Do you think the majority of people would give a similar answer?

WHAT MAKES A HAPPY LIFE?

Listening

2.18 Listen to a lecture in which a professor of psychology talks about the concept of flow. What do the numbers represent on the slide? How would you explain flow in a single sentence?

ACADEMIC KEYWORDS		
passive	(adj)	/'pæsɪv/
positive	(adj)	/'pɑzətɪv/
sense	(n)	/sens/

Factors that accompany a sense of flow

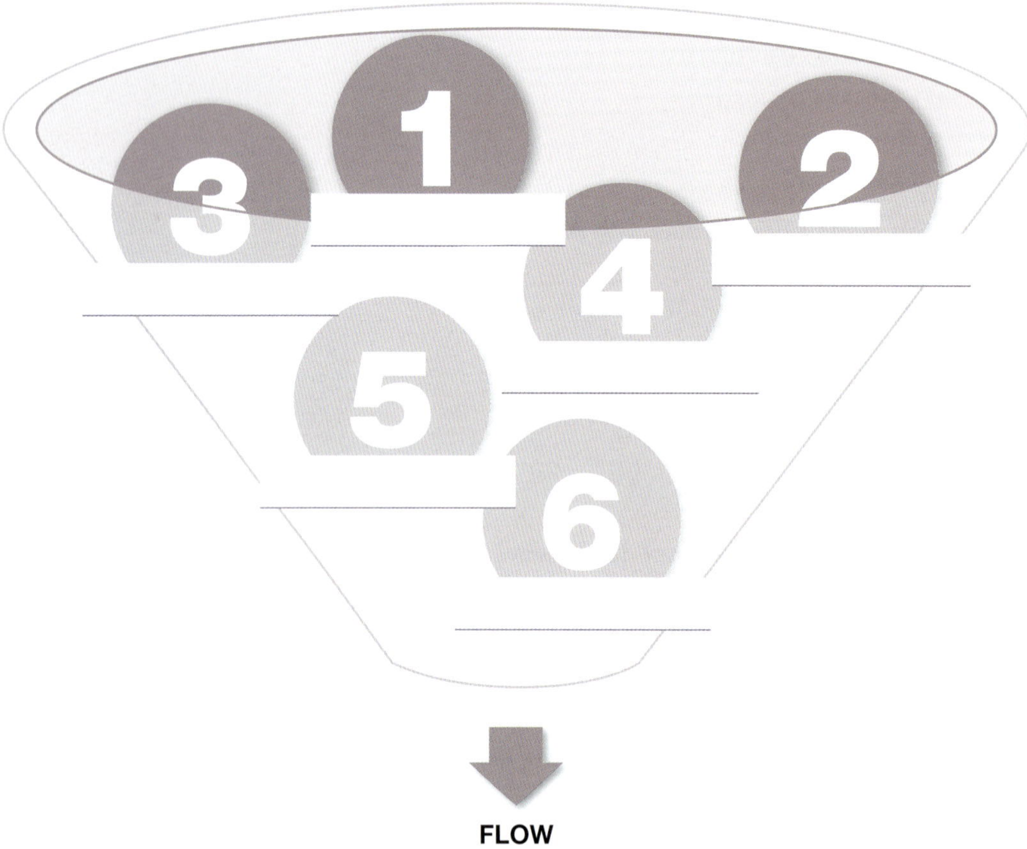

Critical thinking skill

VISUAL AIDS AND DIAGRAMS

Many presentations make use of visual aids and diagrams to help convey ideas and present information. In many cases, the right visual will aid in understanding more than the words. Good presentations will also rely on visual aids to make a memorable impact. It's worth paying attention to visuals and diagrams in lectures to help you remember and think about the content.

1 2.18 **Listen to the lecture again and make some notes about the information each visual aid below conveys.**

1

2

3

4

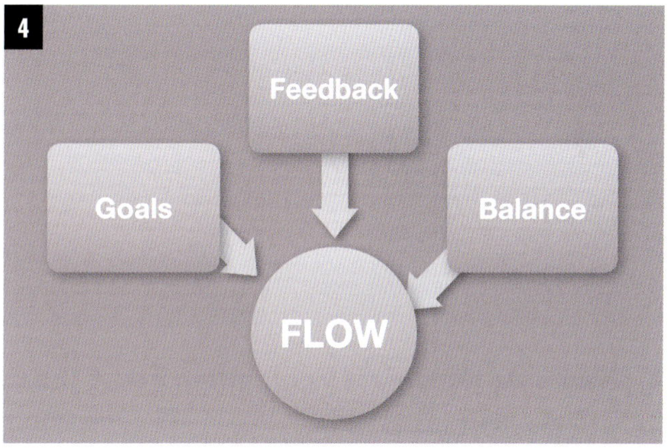

2 2.19 **Listen to the last part of the lecture about the three conditions for flow. Suggest further visual aids that would help make this information easier to remember.**

Developing critical thinking

1 **Discuss these questions in a group.**

1 Have you ever felt in a state of flow? When was it? What were you doing? How did you feel?

2 When people feel creative, they say that ideas "flow." What ways can you help make that happen? What things stop ideas from flowing?

2 **Think about the ideas from *Listening 1* and *Listening 2*, and discuss these questions in a group.**

1 In English, we say that information "flows," just like water. Explain how information can flow. Do you think that information flow is always a good thing? Is it possible to "drown" in too much information?

2 Discuss the advantages and disadvantages of working with other people (for example, on a team project, or as part of a campaigning group) and working alone. Which do you prefer? Why?

Language development

Language development

IRREGULAR PLURALS

In English most nouns have a singular and a plural form, and in the majority of these, the plural form ends with -*s*. However, there are many exceptions.

Some nouns are irregular because of the way the plural is formed. Many of these are familiar, e.g., *foot/feet, man/men,* and *mouse/mice.* Other nouns are irregular because of the way the plural and singular forms are used.

Form	Example
Many words of Latin origin have irregular plural forms. These occur more frequently in academic English, particularly in the sciences.	*crisis/crises, nucleus/nuclei, radius/radii*
Some words have the same plural form as the singular form.	*spacecraft, sheep, deer, fish** *We use fishes when talking about different fish species.
Some words are already plural and have no singular form.	*staff, pants, eyeglasses, groceries, headquarters, crossroads*
Some words have a singular form, but it is not frequently used.	*data* (plural), *datum* (singular)
Some words that refer to groups of people can be considered singular or plural. This depends on whether the speaker sees the group as a collection of individuals or a collective unit.	*My family* ***are*** *all good at languages.* *A family* ***lives*** *in that house.* *The team* ***is*** *going to lose.* *The team* ***are*** *going to lose.*

1 What is the plural of the words below, if any? Use a dictionary to help you.

1 hypothesis ____________
2 series ____________
3 species ____________
4 half ____________
5 basis ____________
6 kilo ____________
7 hero ____________
8 audience ____________
9 proximity ____________
10 metamorphosis ____________
11 stimulus ____________
12 conundrum ____________
13 aircraft ____________
14 bog ____________
15 youth ____________
16 reservoir ____________
17 statistic ____________
18 knowledge ____________

2 Work with a partner. Do these words have a singular form? What is it?

1 groceries ____________
2 criteria ____________
3 cattle ____________
4 knives ____________
5 eyeglasses ____________
6 jeans ____________
7 phenomena ____________
8 physics ____________

3 **Circle the correct word. If both are possible, circle both words.**

1 The data **suggests** / **suggest** that the dam is entirely safe.
2 The police **have closed** / **has closed** the street for the entire day.
3 The committee on environmental issues will give **its** / **their** report at the end of the week.
4 The unemployment statistics **are** / **is** not very good I'm afraid.
5 The bacteria in the sample **is** / **are** multiplying at an exponential rate.
6 The ministry **produce** / **produces** many helpful flowcharts to explain decisions to the public.
7 He was not sure about his hypothesis, so he checked **it** / **them** again, just in case.
8 The United Nations **has** / **have** just announced that next year will be the year of information.
9 The appendices **are** / **is** all in a separate document.
10 The journalists filmed the deer as **it** / **they** fled the rising flood waters.

WORDS IN CONTEXT—WORKING WITH CONCORDANCE DATA

Concordance data is produced by a concordancer. This is a computer program that shows every example of a particular word that is used in a body of text (corpus). Looking at concordance data can help give you more information about word patterns and word frequencies.

has come to light. A	FLOW	of correspondence between the authors
at night there is a continuous	FLOW	of noise from passers-by
allow the free	FLOW	of information to the public via Internet
funds often	FLOW	to the social services during a crisis
adjusts the fuel	FLOW	to the engine of the vehicle
The tunes	FLOW	together nicely on this album
during exercise, the	FLOW	of air from the lungs is increased
stops the	FLOW	of blood to the heart
trying to maintain a	FLOW	of cash to all its clients
enough to stop the blood	FLOW	and reduce the danger
that river water could	FLOW	through. The dam therefore would
has interrupted the	FLOW	of commerce between the countries

Look at the concordance data for the word *flow* and answer the questions.

1 What kind of word is *flow*?
2 What adjectives collocate with *flow*?
3 What things *flow*, apart from water?
4 What common structure occurs with *flow* used as a noun?
5 Which examples of *flow* are associated with the subject of economics?

SPEAKING Making an advertisement supported by visuals

You are going to learn how to use intonation to express hesitation and doubt. You will also learn how to soften criticism when giving feedback on other people's work or ideas. Then you are going to use these skills to make an advertisement supported by visuals.

Pronunciation skill

INTONATION TO EXPRESS HESITATION AND DOUBT

A speaker's intonation can often say much more about whether he or she agrees or disagrees with a point than the actual words that are used. A drawn out *yes* said with a rise-fall intonation can indicate hesitation or doubt, and might actually mean *no*. Similarly, *yes* said with a flat intonation could indicate a reluctance to agree.

1 **Divide the phrases below into two groups: *agree* or *disagree*.**

I don't think so   I guess so   I'm not sure   no   well, OK   yes

2 2.20 **Listen to how each word or phrase is said with different intonation. Does the speaker agree or disagree more strongly in version *a* or in version *b*? Repeat the words and phrases in the different ways.**

Speaking skill

SOFTENING CRITICISM

In academic contexts you may be required to criticize other people's work or ideas. When this occurs in a seminar or discussion, it is important to know how to do this without causing offense. Criticism can be softened in different ways.

- Add a personal evaluation, such as: *I think, I do think, I wonder if …, I (don't) suppose …*
  There's a mistake here. → *I* ***think*** *there's a mistake here.*
  You're not quoting the source correctly. → ***I wonder if*** *you're quoting the source correctly.*
- Use modal verbs, such as: *might* or *may*:
  You're using the wrong book. → *You* ***might*** *be using the wrong book.*
- Use softening phrases to preface a criticism, such as: *It occurs to me (that) …, I might be wrong, but …, It seems to me (that) …*
  The facts presented don't help. → *It* ***seems to me*** *that the facts presented don't help.*

1 **Look at the criticisms. Find two ways to soften each one.**

1 You did the wrong exercise.
2 Your conclusion doesn't make sense.
3 Your accent is very hard to understand.
4 You don't understand what I'm saying.
5 You have to start the whole thing over again.
6 You didn't quote the source correctly.

2 **Share your answers with a partner. Say the sentences.**

3 **Work with a partner. Think of ways you could soften criticism about an aspect of each other's work. Use the topics below and prepare some phrases.**

disorganized notes   distracted in class   incoherent structure
messy handwriting   spelling mistakes   wrong answers to exercises

SPEAKING TASK

BRAINSTORM

Work with a partner. Read this situation. Then answer the questions.

You live in an area that is subject to severe water shortages every year during the summer season. The local government wants to begin a public awareness campaign to encourage the population to conserve water. They are asking for proposals for a 40-second advertisement that will give suggestions on how to save water. This advertisement will be shown on all national television channels.

Here are the kinds of ideas they would like the advertisement to contain:

- Do not leave water running while you wash dishes (fill a sink with water and use that).
- Wash your clothes with a full washing machine load.

Have you ever lived in an area with water shortages? Which of the strategies for saving water mentioned have you used? Think of four or five other ways people can save water and add them to the list.

PLAN

Work individually. Look at your list of strategies for saving water. Which one of these do you think is most important for promoting in a 40-second advertisement? Think about some of the language and images that might fit your strategy.

SPEAK

Work in small groups of three or four. Talk about your ideas for the advertisement and comment on each other's ideas. If you don't agree, use the language you learned in this unit to soften any criticism you make.

As a group, decide on a final advertisement. If you like, design visual aids or produce a storyboard (a series of pictures that the director of a movie uses to plan the action that will be filmed) to go with it. You could also use a tool such as PowerPoint. Draft a voiceover script that might go with your advertisement. Your script should follow the format of introducing your main idea, supporting your points, and providing an effective conclusion, which might be a powerful slogan.

SHARE

Give a presentation of your advertisement in front of the class. Read aloud your voiceover script in the appropriate tone of voice, and explain how the script will fit your visuals. At the end, vote on which advertisement would be the most effective and say why.

Study skills

STUDY SKILLS Exam techniques

Getting started

Discuss these questions with a partner.

1 How do you feel about exams?
2 What are some of the ways that you prepare for an exam?
3 How do you stop yourself feeling nervous before an exam?

Scenario

Read what Tania does before every exam. Which techniques do you think are beneficial?

Tania used to get very nervous every time she had an exam. She would study and study, but on the day of the exam she always felt she had forgotten everything. She spoke with a school counselor about this, and the counselor gave her some tips on what to do before an exam starts so she wouldn't be so nervous.

Tania now focuses on being practical before each exam. She first makes sure she knows exactly where the exam will take place, and she visits the room before, if possible. She leaves much earlier to get to the exam. She always brings a special "exam kit" with her, which has spare pens, pencils, and a bottle of water, if it's allowed.

She doesn't take notes with her to the exam unless there is somewhere safe she can leave them when she gets there. She tries to stay positive, and avoids other students and people who make her feel nervous and anxious about exams. Finally, she always tries to get a good night's sleep before the exam.

Tania still doesn't enjoy exams, but these routines have helped calm her nerves before she takes an exam.

Consider it

Look at these tips for what to do during an exam. Do you do any of these things?

1 **Make a note of the time that you must move on to the next question.**
It's easier to pass if you answer the right number of questions rather than running out of time because you spend too long on one question.
2 **Read the questions slowly and highlight key points.**
Make sure you really understand what each question says. It's easy to misread a question or miss parts of a question in an exam.
3 **Check the back of the paper to see if there are other questions.**
Many people forget to do this!
4 **Structure your answers just as you would for coursework.**
5 **If you go blank, brainstorm words and ideas on a sheet of notepaper.**
These will eventually stimulate your ideas. Move on to the next question that you can do rather than staying stuck on the same problem. The information will probably come back to you later.
6 **Check through your work at the end.**
You might even try reading it to yourself, mouthing the words. You may find parts that do not make sense because you have left out a key word or key point. Add these in neatly at the end of the page.

Over to you

Discuss these questions with a partner.

1 Which of the things in *Consider it* do you think you do already? Which do you think you would benefit from doing?
2 Do you have any other tips or techniques for *before* or *during* exams?
3 Is there anything you do or avoid doing *after* an exam has finished?

Conflict

CRITICAL THINKING	Identifying strengths in theories and arguments Consistency
LANGUAGE DEVELOPMENT	Hedging and boosting Using the correct linker
PRONUNCIATION	Linking and catenation
SPEAKING	Managing conflict—reformulating and monitoring

Discussion point

Discuss these questions with a partner.

1 How many different kinds of conflict between the following pairs can you think of? Can you think of specific examples for each one?

human		human
nature	vs.	nature
machine		machine

2 When you think of conflict, is it always associated with negative thoughts? Can conflict ever be a positive thing?

3 What kinds of conflict do you experience in your day-to-day life? How do you deal with them?

Vocabulary preview

1 Complete these sentences with the words in the box.

accusation	aftermath	alluding to	animosity	
criticize	loyalty	rivalry	struggle	violent

1 The speaker didn't say it directly, but she was ______________ how difficult it is to ______________ different nationalities.
2 The local authorities had to deal with thousands of homeless families in the ______________ of the flood.
3 There was always a strong ______________ between students at the city's two universities, but never any real ______________.
4 He was expelled from the school for ______________ behavior.
5 His ______________ makes me think that he will not go against his brother's decision.
6 The athlete faced a long and difficult ______________ to get fit again after suffering a serious injury.
7 Sharmila faced an ______________ of plagiarism after she failed to credit her sources in an essay.

2 Which of the words in the box are usually used in negative situations? Which words are positive or neutral?

LISTENING 1 Conflict of interest

Before you listen

1 An abstract is a summary of a talk or a paper. Read the abstract from a talk at a leadership conference and choose the best title.

> Have you ever heard the expression "good guys finish last"? It's often used to justify why making a morally wrong choice helps people get ahead in life. In my talk, I'll show you why ethical dilemmas are so problematic and give you frameworks to show you how to make the right choices on a path towards success.

a A framework for making the right choice
b Avoid moral conflicts of interest and still be successful!
c Do good guys always finish last?

2 Can you think of an example situation that supports the statement "good guys finish last"? Then think of an example that disproves it.

ACADEMIC KEYWORDS

outcome	(n)	/ˈaʊtˌkʌm/
internal	(adj)	/ɪnˈtɜrn(ə)l/
treat	(v)	/trit/

Listening

2.21 Listen to the beginning of the leadership conference talk and look at the headings in a participant's notes. Why are the following words and phrases mentioned? With a partner, take turns summarizing the sections.

ugly baby *scholarship applicant* *consequential and non-consequential*
closing the factory *justice, generosity, loyalty*

Critical thinking skill

IDENTIFYING STRENGTHS IN THEORIES AND ARGUMENTS

Being a critical thinker means you should not only be able to identify weaknesses in arguments or theories presented to you, but you should also be able to recognize strengths. This helps you reach a more balanced decision about what information you select or reject. To do this, you should evaluate the following:

	Strong argument	**Weak argument**
Are the arguments based on …?	facts reasonable assumptions	speculation unreasonable assumptions / generalizations
Identify the sources. Is the evidence supporting the argument …?	sufficient valid reliable relevant	insufficient invalid unreliable irrelevant
Do the arguments and evidence support each other logically?	yes	no

assumption = something you consider to be true even though you have no proof

speculation = an idea that may be possible, but is not necessarily likely

generalization = a statement that is claimed to be true in most situations, but is not based on enough evidence

1 2.21 **Listen again and complete each of the following theories with a word in the box.**

egotistical golden rule *prima facie* utilitarian

1. A choice that produces a good result for the largest number of people is based on a ______________ theory.
2. The ______________ theory says that you should act towards others as you would like them to act towards you.
3. A theory that states that you should do the right thing if it produces a good result for you is ______________.
4. The ______________ duties say that a choice is the right one if you make it while following certain principles, such as justice or generosity.

2 **Read the possible criticisms of each of the theories in exercise 1. Which theory is each one criticizing?**

a. Others may feel differently than me about how they want to be treated. ___
b. This theory ignores the interests of others and means you are selfish. ___
c. If I use this theory to make a difficult choice, and two duties are in conflict with each other, how do I know which one to follow? ___
d. The problem with this theory is that something may be good for the majority of people, but still be wrong. ___

Developing critical thinking

Discuss these questions in a group.

1. Consider the two dilemmas presented in the talk. What would you do in each case? Which theory applies best to each? Why?
2. Think of a moral conflict that you have experienced. How was it resolved? Which theory might have helped resolve it more easily?

LISTENING 2 "The Sporting Spirit"

Before you listen

1 Discuss these questions with a partner.

1 Have you been to a major international sporting event? What was the atmosphere like?

2 Think of three big sporting events in your country. Are there any famous rivalries? What are they? How does the news cover these events?

2 Read about an essay written by George Orwell and answer these questions.

1 Does the essay present a positive or negative view of sports?

2 Find two synonyms of *attack/criticize*.

3 After reading this description, do you think the essay is likely to give a balanced or one-sided view?

The famous British novelist, George Orwell, is perhaps best known for his books *Animal Farm* and *1984*, but he was also a critical commentator on life and politics in the twentieth century. One of his most famous essays was called "The Sporting Spirit."

"The Sporting Spirit" was written in 1945. In it, Orwell lashes out at the competitive nature of sports between nations. He cites the example of an English–Soviet soccer game designed to improve relations between the countries, which instead worsened them. In the essay, he goes on to lambast other forms of sports that, when played between countries, cause negative feelings of nationalism to emerge.

In Orwell's words, "*Sport is an unfailing cause of ill will … Serious sport has nothing to do with fair play. It is bound up with hatred, jealousy, boastfulness, disregard of all rules, and sadistic pleasure in witnessing violence: in other words it is war minus the shooting.*"

Listening

2.22 **Listen to a seminar in which a professor and students are discussing George Orwell's essay "The Sporting Spirit." Number the events in order.**

a A brief summary of the article is given. ____

b Evidence is provided which goes against the statement. ____

c Evidence is provided which supports the statement. ____

d The context of the essay is described. ____

e The professor tries to get the group to reach a conclusion. ____

f There is debate on what the author meant. ____

ACADEMIC KEYWORDS

essence	(n)	/ˈesəns/
mutual	(adj)	/ˈmjutʃuəl/
precede	(v)	/prɪˈsid/

Critical thinking skill

CONSISTENCY

A well-structured argument should be consistent; in other words, all the main lines of reasoning should agree with each other and lead to the conclusion. Nothing should contradict or undermine the main message. Detecting inconsistencies in an argument helps you to evaluate how good it is and to think critically about opposing views.

Be careful—if an element of the argument doesn't link to the conclusion, that doesn't always mean it is an inconsistency. Some information is incidental; in other words, background information. This does not have to support the conclusion directly, but it should not contradict it either.

A speaker will sometimes present arguments that oppose his conclusion—this does not affect the consistency of his argument if she or he then presents a counter-argument. If there is no counter-argument, this is an inconsistency.

1 2.22 **Listen again to the seminar. Which elements mentioned by the students are consistent with Orwell's conclusion that "Sport is an unfailing cause of ill will"? Put ✓ next to them. Which ones could contradict the conclusion? Put ✗ next to them. Put *I* next to any information that is incidental.**

1 ☐ There were negative feelings between the two countries before the sporting event.

2 ☐ Soccer is a competitive sport. There can only be one winner and one loser.

3 ☐ The Olympic Games® were founded on the philosophy that the important thing is not the triumph, but the struggle.

4 ☐ The players on both teams acted violently during the game.

5 ☐ The crowd was aggressive towards the players and the referee.

6 ☐ Nationalist feelings come out at big rival sporting events.

2 **At the end of the seminar, the students feel that the author has contradicted himself, and that therefore his argument is inconsistent. What example do they give?**

Developing critical thinking

1 **Discuss these questions in a group.**

1 Do you agree with Orwell? Think of one example of your own that supports his argument and one example that goes against it.

2 Apart from sports, are there other good ways that countries can come together for international events that everyone enjoys? Think of one possible example.

2 **Think about the ideas from *Listening 1* and *Listening 2*, and discuss these questions in a group.**

1 Think back to the idea of moral dilemmas in the first listening. What are some common ethical dilemmas in the world of sports? Think about: athlete salaries, recruiting players from other countries, the use of performance-enhancing drugs, ...

2 If it's true that competitive sports are not always a good thing, why do you think they are nonetheless so popular?

Language development

Language development

HEDGING AND BOOSTING

In academic discourse, it is common to avoid making claims and statements very assertive. It is less common, but also sometimes necessary, to assert a claim quite directly. These processes are called hedging (less assertive claim) and boosting (more assertive claim).

Hedging

Can, could, might, and *may* are less assertive modal verbs. (cf. p. 13)

*We **could** say this is a typical occurrence.*

Hedging language also includes:

- certain verbs: *assume, appear …*
- adverbs of frequency: *often, sometimes …*
- adverbs of probability: *arguably, probably …*
- determiners: *some, many …*
- approximating language: *roughly (speaking), more* or *less …*

  *It is **arguably** the most difficult of moral choices to make.*

  ***More or less** every country on the planet is engaged in one conflict or another.*

Boosting

Will and *must* are more assertive.

*We **must** remember that these conflicts could erupt at any moment.*

*When faced with such a dilemma, people **will** always choose the option that brings the greatest personal benefit.*

Boosting language also includes:

- adverbs of probability: *undeniably, absolutely …*
- determiners: *all, every, each*
- some fixed expressions: *There is no question …, If one thing is certain …*

  *It's **undeniably** the most potent threat we have ever faced.*

  ***There is no doubt** that the majority of people would choose the first option.*

1 Decide if the following expressions can be used to make a statement more assertive (+) or less assertive (–).

apparently	as a general rule	categorically
certainly	for certain	in a sense
in some respects	inevitably	likely
partially	seemingly	unquestionably
without a doubt		

2 Look at the following statements. If the statement contains hedging, change it so it is more assertive. If it contains boosting, change it so it is less assertive.

1 Now, this is a rather small dilemma, and it's probably easy for most people to solve it.

2 An action that produces a good result must be morally right.

3 Faced with difficult choices and internal conflict, these frameworks, I believe, clearly help us.

4 We must remind ourselves that without electricity, nothing would work.

5 The threat is out there, and it's undeniably real.

3 **Choose two of the sentences below. Adjust them so they reflect your opinion, using boosting or hedging language.**

1 Sports are good for your health.
2 If left to themselves, people do the right thing.
3 Modern sports are all about the money and not really about the sport.
4 Globalization causes more good will than ill will.

Language development

USING THE CORRECT LINKER

Linkers show transition between points in an argument, signal concepts such as counter-argument, and signpost the structure of a lecture or presentation.

Firstly and *At first*

Firstly is used to talk about the first thing in a list.

*Let's begin **firstly** with consequential theories.*

At first is often used to contrast two different situations in time.

***At first** I was unsure, but I grew more confident with time.*

Lastly and *At last*

Lastly is used to talk about the last thing in a list.

*We'll discuss the current threats, then solutions, and **lastly** we will put this in a historical perspective of different kinds of conflict.*

At last is used to indicate that something happened, but later than was hoped.

*The company began making preparations **at last**, but many feared it was already too late.*

On the contrary and *On the other hand*

On the contrary rejects a previous statement for a different one.

*The truth is most of us don't consider other people's interests before our own. **On the contrary**, we tend to be selfish.*

On the other hand is used to compare or contrast two statements.

*You believe honesty is important. **On the other hand**, you don't want to hurt your friend's feelings.*

1 **Underline the correct linkers.**

1 There were many factors that led to this conflict. **Firstly / At first** the location of the disputed territory, right on the border of the two countries, was problematic.
2 We had **firstly / at first** been expecting a much more difficult experience, and so we were relieved when it all went well.
3 In 1985 the company got rid of its typewriters. The digital age had arrived **at last / lastly**.
4 We have no intention of harming anyone. **On the contrary / On the other hand**, we come in peace.
5 The loyal forces were well equipped and had the support of the people. The rebels, **on the contrary / on the other hand**, were struggling to survive.

2 **Finish the sentences below with your own ideas.**

1 I remember my first day at this school. At first …
2 The Internet gives us unlimited access to information. On the other hand …
3 I don't enjoy conflict. On the contrary …
4 In my next paper I will firstly …

SPEAKING Role-playing mini-conflict situations

You are going to practice linking and sentence stress in longer utterances. You are going to look at how reformulating and monitoring what you say can help manage conflicts and arguments. Then you are going to use these skills to role-play a series of mini-conflict situations.

Pronunciation skill

LINKING AND CATENATION

Catenation is the process of linking the final consonant sound of a word with the opening vowel sound of the following word. Fluent speakers do this regularly. When listening to fluent speech there can be examples of catenation that cause confusion as the words run together.

I'm having ***a nice cold*** *drink.* → *I'm having* ***an ice cold*** *drink.*

1 **Say the words in the box. Then read the sentences below. Can you find the same pronunciation of the words in the box within the sentences below?**

doubt	sand	sit	tab	tall	tie

1 I'd like to offer frameworks and theories.
2 I see your point about this.
3 That exam was awful—if I pass it, I'll be amazed.
4 Nothing at all.
5 The team walked out of the stadium.
6 I'd like to say that I agree.

2 2.23 **Compare your pronunciation of the sentences in exercise 1 with an American English speaker.**

Speaking skill

MANAGING CONFLICT—REFORMULATING AND MONITORING

When two speakers are having a disagreement or are in conflict, they may try to restate their own arguments or the other speaker's arguments in a different way, using the following phrases: *in other words, to put it another way, as it were, so you're saying …*

Other markers indicate that the speaker is correcting something incorrect that the other speaker said or implied: *actually, strictly speaking, technically, as a matter of fact …*

1 2.24 **Listen to a discussion between two students. What is the problem? What happens in the end?**

2 2.24 **Listen again. Notice the ways the speakers reformulate and monitor their discourse.**

3 **Work with a partner. Start the exchange and continue the discussion. Use appropriate phrases to manage your "conflict."**

A: Do you think you could turn off your music?
B: I like listening to the radio when I study.
A: But it's very loud.

SPEAKING TASK

BRAINSTORM

1 **Look at the following conflict situations. Which ones do you think are most common? Have you ever been in similar situations?**

1. Abdulaziz and Hakan are students in a university dormitory. Hakan makes a lot of noise in his room at night. Abdulaziz can't study because of the noise.
2. Carla and Victoria are working on an important project together. Carla often shows up late for meetings, and sometimes doesn't come at all.
3. Özge and Jennifer are both academics in the same field. Özge discovers that Jennifer has published a paper on exactly the same topic Özge wanted to write about. Özge suspects Jennifer stole her ideas.
4. Tran and Graham are friends. Graham wants Tran to join a social network online so they can stay in touch. Tran doesn't trust the Internet or social networks.

PLAN

1 Work in a group of three. Choose a conflict from the brainstorm section.

2 Assign roles. Student A plays the role of the first character in the confict. Student B plays the role of the other character. Student C is the arbitrator. The arbitrator is responsible for trying to help A and B come to an agreement. Prepare some phrases that you anticipate you will need in your role. Think about how you will identify the strengths and weaknesses of the other person's argument, detecting inconsistencies. Try to incorporate hedging linkers, reformulating, and correcting.

SPEAK

Perform your role play. Each person should talk for an equal amount of time. Pay attention to reformulating and monitoring the progression of the argument.

SHARE

Work with another group. Tell each other what situation you role-played and if and how you came to a resolution. How much of a role did the arbitrator play in reaching the resolution in each case? Did you feel that the resolution you reached genuinely reflected how you would have handled the situation in real life?

Categorising

by Stella Cottrell

Categorising skills are important to critical thinking as they enable you to sort information into appropriate groups and recognise which information has relevant connections to other kinds of information. In critical analysis, this helps you to compare the right things, so that you compare 'like with like'. This is necessary for constructing sophisticated arguments, such as in debate or for essays and reports.

Comparisons

Drawing comparisons is essentially about finding similarities and identifying differences. The same two items may be considered to be similar or different depending on the context and the criteria used for comparison, as the following set of questions demonstrates.

Q1 What do these eight items have in common?

zebra	cat	puppy	goldfish
whale	kitten	seal	elephant

Q2 What do these items have in common which makes them different from the other items in the list in Q1?

cat goldfish kitten puppy

Q3 What do these items have in common which makes them different from other items in the list?

kitten puppy

The items in Q1 are all animals. Q2 has focused in on animals that are common domestic pets and Q3, on *young* domestic pets. In each case, the selection focuses in more detail on a narrower range of shared characteristics.

Salient characteristics

'Salient' simply means 'relevant to the argument'. In the above examples, your existing knowledge of animals and pets probably made it easy to recognise the characteristics that the items in each group shared. When you recognise the characteristics that a set of items holds in common then, in effect, you are sorting these into groups, or categorising. A category is simply a group of items with shared characteristics. Any kind of category is possible: tall pointed objects; green vegetables; current prime ministers.

Activity: Categorising

Identify the following categories (in other words, what does each group have in common?).

(a) pond lake sea pool
(b) Indian Irish Icelandic Bolivian
(c) lair den pen burrow hutch
(d) biology chemistry physics geology
(e) creates stellar engines soothes
(f) decide deliver denounce devour
(g) never seven cleverest severe
(h) memory language problem-solving
(i) appendicitis tonsillitis colonitis
(j) rotor minim deed peep tenet
(k) cheluviation illuviation leaching salination
(l) 21 35 56 84 91
(m) oligarchy exarchy plutarchy democracy
(n) cete herd colony flock drove

Categorising involves not merely identifying shared salient characteristics, but also having the right background knowledge and vocabulary to label the group once identified. You may have found this an issue when trying to describe some of the groups above. Good background knowledge and vocabulary do make it easier to find, sort and use information at speed, making critical thinking more efficient. The above items were easier to categorise because you already knew that they formed a category. This meant you only had to find the salient characteristics of ready-formed groups. Pattern-finding skills also make it easier to identify similarities when a group is not already pre-formed.

Functional language

The phrases below give common ways of expressing useful functions. Use them to help you as you're completing the *Discussion points* and *Developing critical thinking* activities.

Asking for clarification

Sorry, can you explain that some more?
Could you say that another way?
When you say ..., do you mean ...?
Sorry, I don't follow that.
What do you mean?

Asking for repetition

Could you repeat that, please?
I'm sorry, I didn't catch that.
Could you say that again?

When you don't know the meaning of a word

What does ... mean?
Sorry, I'm not sure what ... means.

Working with a partner

Would you like to start?
Shall I go first?
Shall we do this one first?
Where do you want to begin?

Giving opinions

I think that ...
It seems to me that ...
In my opinion ...
As I see it ...

Agreeing and disagreeing

I know what you mean.
That's true.
You have a point there.
Yes. I see what you're saying, but ...
I understand your point, but ...
I don't think that's true.

Asking for opinions

Do you think ...?
Do you feel ...?
What do you think about ...?
How about you, Jennifer? What do you think?
What about you?
Does anyone have any other ideas?
Do you have any thoughts on this?

Asking for more information

In what way?
Why do you think that?
Can you give an example?

Not giving a strong preference

It doesn't matter to me.
I don't really have a strong preference.
I've never really thought about that.
Either is fine.

Expressing interest

I'd like to hear more about that.
That sounds interesting.
How interesting!
Tell me more about that.

Giving reasons

This is ... because ...
This has to be ... because ...
I think ... because ...

Checking understanding

Do you know what I mean?
Do you see what I'm saying?
Are you following me?

Putting things in order

This needs to come first because ...
I think this is the most/least important because ...
For me, this is the most/least relevant because ...

Preventing interruptions

Excuse me, I wasn't finished.
If I could just finish what I was saying ...
Let me just finish this, please.
I haven't finished my thought/sentence.

Buying time

Let me think about that for a moment.
Let me gather my thoughts.
Just a minute. I need to think about that.

Clarifying

That's not exactly what I meant.
Sorry, I wasn't clear. Let me put it another way.
That isn't what I was trying to say.

Reviewers

The publishers would like to thank the following for their thoughtful insights and perceptive comments during the development of the material:

Belgium

Sylviane Granger, at CECL, University of Louvain

Magali Paquot

Egypt

Dr. Gaber Khalil, AUC, Cairo

Heidi Omara

Germany

John Nixon at Universität Stuttgart

Ireland

Fiodhna Gardiner-Hyland at University of Limerick

Japan

Robert Morton at Chuo University

Lesley Burda Ito

Oman

Mutaz Abumuaath at Nizwa College of Technology, Nizwa

Qatar

Jane Hoelker at Qatar University, Foundation English

Russia

Tatyana Gromoglasova, at the Siberian Institute of Management, Novosibirsk

Saudi Arabia

Dr. Mohammed Al-Ahaydib and Dr Mohammed Hamdan at Imam Muhammad Ibn Saud University

Dr. William Frawley, Education Experts

South Korea

Yoonji Kim, and Da Young Song at the Konkuk University Language Institute

Jina Kwon at Seoul National University

Taiwan

Laura Wang at Chung Yuan Christian University

Regina Jan at Lunghwa University of Science and Technology

Kitty Chu, Jessie Huang, Jenny Jen, and Wenyau Keng at the National Central University, Language Center

Sandrine Ting at the Department of Applied Foreign Language, St. John's University

Thailand

Wanpen Chaikitmongkol, Jindarat De Vleeschauwer, and Sonhsi Wichaidit at the English Division, Department of Western Languages and Humanities, Chiang Mai University

Turkey

Merve Oflaz at Bahçeşehir University

Şahika Özkan-Tuğba Kın-Yadigar Aslan, Didem Gümüşlüoğlu, Meltem Sarandal, and Sibel Weeks at Doğuş University, İstanbul

Sevil Altıkulaçoğlu, Sühendan Semine Er, Şerife Ersöz, and Fatma Ünveren Gürocak at Gazi University

Deniz Ateşok at Istanbul Bilgi University

Ebru Yamaç at Maltepe University

Aybike Oğuz at Özyeğin University

United Arab Emirates

Paul Barney, Doug Henderson, and Danielle Norris at Higher Colleges of Technology, Al Ain

United Kingdom

Nick Hillman at Anglia Ruskin University

Heather Abel and Richard Hillman at Bell London

Edward Bressan, Sara Hannam, and Stacey Hughes at Oxford Brookes University

Sally Morris, Ian Pople, and Simon Raw at University of Manchester

Averil Bolster and Peter Levrai at University of Nottingham, Ningbo

Jonathan Hadley

Jane Neill at University of Gloucester

United States

Gail Schafers at Fontbonne University

Carole Mawson at Stanford University

Denise Mussman at University of Missouri

Abby Brown

Macmillan Education
4 Crinan Street London N1 9XW
A division of Macmillan Publishers Limited
Companies and representatives throughout the world

ISBN 978-1-786-32209-8

Written by Lindsay Clandfield and Mark McKinnon
Series Consultant Dorothy E. Zemach

This edition published 2016
First published 2014

Designed by emc design ltd
Illustrated by emc design ltd
Cover design by emc design ltd
Cover illustration/photograph by Thinkstock/iStockphoto
Picture research by Emily Taylor

The Academic Keyword List (AKL) was designed by Magali Paquot at the Centre for English Corpus Linguistics, Université catholique de Louvain (Belgium) within the framework of a research project led by Professor Sylviane Granger.

http://www.uclouvain.be/en-372126.html

Authors' acknowledgements

Lindsay Clandfield
I would like to thank the team at Macmillan for all their work and support on this project, and as always a special thanks to my wife Sofia and children Lucas and Marcos. I am also very happy to have worked with co-author Mark McKinnon on this project.

Mark McKinnon
I would like to thank the Macmillan editorial team for their excellent support during the writing process. I am grateful to Lindsay Clandfield for our brainstorming sessions and his inspiration. A big thank you to my wife Almudena for her understanding and encouragement throughout. I'd also like to thank Mum, Dad, Richard, and Mhairi for helping me get to where I am today. Finally, I'd like to dedicate this book to all the teachers, trainers and trainees that I have worked with throughout my career.

The authors and publishers would like to thank the following for permission to reproduce their photographs:

Alamy/Arcade Images p18, Alamy/Asia File p45(2), Alamy/Michael Doolittle p33, Alamy/EPA p60(bl), Alamy/Horizons WWP p68, Alamy/Image Source p76, Alamy/Pictorial Press Ltd p60(br), Alamy/Pixsooz p35;
Awl Images/Michele Falzone pp67, 75, Awl Images/Travel Pix Collection p58;
Axiom/Peter McBride/Aurora Photos p57;
Corbis/Blend Images p42, Corbis/Bloomimage p22, Corbis/Peer Grimm/DPA p60(bm), Corbis/Hill Street Studios/Blend Images p85, Corbis/Frans Lanting p97, Corbis/Joe McDonald p78(br), Corbis/Moodboard p82, Corbis/John Norris pp5(tl),70-71, Corbis/Celia Peterson p16, Corbis/Anderson Ross/Blend Images pp15, 36, Corbis/Arial Skelley p8;
Fotolibra/Mark Ferguson p40;
Getty Images p45(3), Getty Images/AFP pp37, 95, Getty Images/Amana Images p63, Getty Images/Bloomimage p105(cr), Getty Images/Peter Cade p28, Getty Images/Gallo Images ROOTS Collection p72, Getty Images/Image Source p45(1), Getty Images/Jetta Productions p98, Getty Images/Jonathan Kirn p80, Getty Images/Frans Lemmens p20, Getty Images/Lonely Planet Images p50(br), Getty Images/National Geographic p78(bl), Getty Images/PhotoTalk p56, Getty Images/The Image Bank p88, Getty Images/VCL/Alistair Berg p105(cl), Getty Images/Dimitri Vervitsiotis p91(1), Getty Images/Hiroshi Watanabe p55, Getty Images/Westend61 p52;
Macmillan Mexico p60(tl);
Plain Picture p65, Plain Picture/Amanaimages p47, Plain Picture/Apply Pictures p7, Plain Picture/Atomara p87, Plain Picture/Cultura p50(tr), Plain Picture/Fancy Images p96, Plain Picture/Robert Harding p48, Plain Picture/Image Source p91(2), Plain Picture/Johner p103, Plain Picture/Kerstin Koletzki p27, Plain Picture/Maskot p30, Plain Picture/Minden Pictures pp5(br),77, Plain Picture/Photoalto p25;
Press Association Images/AP pp17, 100;
Rex Features/KeystoneUSA-ZUMA p38, Rex Features/Quirky China News p10;
Stockbyte p12, Stoc\kbyte/Punchstock p91(3).

The authors and publishers are grateful for permission to reprint the following copyright material:

Material from *Critical Thinking Skills 2nd ed'n* 2011 by author Stella Cottrell, copyright © Stella Cottrell 2011, first published by Palgrave Macmillan 2005, reproduced with permission of the publisher;

Direct quotation by Professor Paul Bedford, reprinted with approval;

Material by Miles and Jenkins reprinted with approval of Dr. Jo Saunders;

Material from The Sporting Spirit from 'SHOOTING AN ELEPHANT AND OTHER ESSAYS' by George Orwell. Copyright © 1950 by Sonia Brownell Orwell. Copyright © renewed 1978 by Sonia Pitt-Rivers. Used by permission of Houghton Mifflin Harcourt Publishing Company USA. All rights reserved.

"*The Sporting Spirit*" by George Orwell (Copyright © George Orwell). Reprinted by permission of Bill Hamilton as the Literary Executor of the Estate of the Late Sonia Brownell Orwell.

Printed and bound in Thailand

2020 2019 2018 2017 2016
10 9 8 7 6 5 4 3 2 1